"If prototyping isn't already part of your design process, this book will not only persuade you that it should be, but will also show you how to make it happen. Todd's straightforward explanations and useful examples will help even experienced designers decide what kind of prototyping to do, when to do it, and what tools will be most effective. When someone asks me about prototyping, I'll be pointing them to this book from now on."

—Kim Goodwin
VP Design, Cooper and author, *Designing for the Digital Age*

"One quarter of the way through this book, we threw out our requirements docs and started using photos of our whiteboard sketches to communicate instead. Thanks to Todd for consolidating and analyzing the wisdom and case studies from a variety of practitioners to identify what prototyping techniques will work, now."

—Shaun Abrahamson
Innovator and Investor, Colaboratorie Mutopo

"Todd's text offers a comprehensive view of prototyping—from the role of prototypes in socializing decision making and achieving organizational buy-in, to the actual pragmatics of creating interactive artifacts. This is a solid book for those "in the trenches"—the designers doing the actual work that ends up in the actual products we use every day."

—Jon Kolko
Editor-in-Chief, *interactions* and Associate Creative Director, Frog

ix

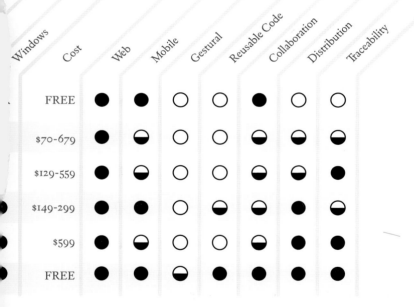

Methods & Tools Comparison Matr

Use this chart to help you select the right method or tool for your next project.

	Paper	Digital	Narrative	Interactive	Rapid	Early	Late	Mac	N
Paper	●	◐	●	◐	●	●	◐	N/A	N
PowerPoint/Keynote	◐	◐	●	◐	●	●	◐	●	●
Visio	●	◐	●	◐	●	●	◐	N/A	●
Fireworks	◐	●	●	●	●	●	●	●	●
Axure RP Pro	◐	●	●	●	●	●	●	N/A	●
HTML	◐	●	●	●	●	●	●	●	●

HOW TO READ THIS TABLE

● Ideal   ◐ Capable, but Not Ideal   ○ Not Suitable

Prototyping: A Practitioner's Guide, Todd Zaki Warfel, Rosenfeld Media, ISBN: 1-933820-21

"If you design applications and are stuck in the land of task flows and wireframes, you really need to pick up a copy of Prototyping: A Practitioner's Guide. Todd offers practical, hands-on advice to jump-start your prototyping and make your designs truly interactive before they are built."

—Dan Saffer
Principal, Kicker Studios and author of
Designing for Interaction and *Designing Gestural Interfaces*

"A major contribution to the field, Todd Zaki Warfel's book perfectly balances know-why and know-how. He uses great cases to help you understand why prototyping is so powerful, and he gives you the tools and techniques to apply the ideas immediately in your own practice."

—Chris Conley
Founding Director, Gravity Tank

"Whether you're prototyping to explore ideas or to communicate them, Todd Zaki Warfel's smart, accessible guide will give you the tools you need."

—Jesse James Garrett
Author, *The Elements of User Experience* and President, Adaptive Path

"Todd tackles the biggest questions of prototyping—for example, how detailed? what form?—with the grand principles and practical examples necessary for success. I wish I'd had this book years ago."

—Bill DeRouchey
Senior Interaction Designer, Ziba Design

PROTOTYPING
A PRACTITIONER'S GUIDE

Todd Zaki Warfel

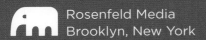

Rosenfeld Media
Brooklyn, New York

Prototyping: A Practitioner's Guide
By Todd Zaki Warfel

Rosenfeld Media, LLC
457 Third Street, #4R
Brooklyn, New York, 11215
USA

On the Web: www.rosenfeldmedia.com
Please send errors to: errata@rosenfeldmedia.com

Publisher: Louis Rosenfeld
Editor/Production Editor: Marta Justak
Interior Layout Tech: Danielle Foster
Cover Design: The Heads of State
Indexer: Nancy Guenther
Proofreader: Sue Boshers

HOW TO USE THIS BOOK

There are countless books on how to code HTML, CSS, and JavaScript. There's also no shortage of software development books on how to program in Java, .Net, PHP, Python, or Ruby on Rails. Looking for a book on using Flash, Dreamweaver, Photoshop, or Visio to design interfaces? Yup, we've got those in spades, too.

What we lack is a short, yet comprehensive book focused solely on prototyping for user experience practitioners. That is until now.

This book is a mix of foundational prototyping theory and practical how-tos. I've included a number of real-world case studies, some from my own work and some from other practitioners in the field. I've also packed the book with a number of tips that will help you prototype faster, easier, and with greater success.

Who Should Read This Book?

This book is written for anyone involved in the design or development of a product or service. If you're a visual designer, interaction designer, information architect, developer, usability engineer, product manager, or business owner, this book will show you how to leverage prototyping to improve communication within your company and avoid costly mistakes.

What's in This Book?

This book is organized into three main sections.

Section One. The first five chapters provide foundational theory and best practices for prototyping. You'll even find a few guidelines for selecting a prototyping method best suited for your needs.

Section Two. The next six chapters discuss specific methods of prototyping—from paper prototyping to coded HTML. Each chapter starts with a matrix, showing how the specific method measures up, based on a number of important characteristics. Next, you'll find a summary of the method's strengths and weakness. Finally, each chapter provides a step-by-step guided how-to prototyping tutorial packed with tips and tricks.

Section Three. The last chapter in the book will guide you through the actual process of testing your prototype.

What Comes with This Book?

This book's companion Web site (🐘 rosenfeldmedia.com/books/prototyping) contains links to a number of prototyping resources, including articles, videos, tools, templates, and example files referenced in this book. You can also find a calendar of my upcoming talks on prototyping and a place to engage others in conversations about prototyping.

We've also made the book's diagrams, screenshots, and other illustrations available under a Creative Common license for you to download and include in your own presentations. You can find these on Flickr at 🐘 www.flickr.com/photos/rosenfeldmedia/sets/.

FREQUENTLY
ASKED QUESTIONS

What prototyping method should I use?

When choosing a prototyping method, a number of deciding factors need to be considered. You should start by asking the following questions: What's the goal of this prototype? Who is its audience? How comfortable am I with this method? Is it something I already know or can learn quickly? How effective will this method be at helping me communicate or test my design? The right prototyping method for your current situation depends on how you answer these questions. As your answers change, so might your selection of prototyping methods and tools. See Chapter 5.

Hi-fidelity or lo-fidelity?

Neither. Prototype fidelity is a sliding scale. Don't be concerned with hi-level or lo-level fidelity. The level of fidelity that matters is whatever is needed to help you accomplish your goal with the audience for your prototype. See page 44.

What are the differences between a wireframe, storyboard, and a prototype?

A prototype, regardless of its fidelity, functionality, or how it is made, captures the intent of a design and simulates multiple states of that design. Wireframes and storyboards are static representations of a design that on their own merit do not simulate multiple states of a design. It's the *simulation* and *multiple states* part that creates the distinction. See pages 3-4.

Why isn't "tool x" in your book?

I chose to include tools that were widely used in the field of user experience. When I started this book, I surveyed a few hundred practitioners to get a feel for the most common tools being used in the field of user experience. You can find the results of that survey in Chapter 5, "Picking the Right Tool."

Some tools, like Flash, have entire books dedicated to them. Flash is a great prototyping tool, but because it is so popular, I felt other tools deserved more attention.

OmniGraffle and Balsamiq are great diagramming tools that can be used for prototyping, but at the time of this book, neither represented a large enough market share to warrant writing about them. That might change. I'll be watching.

How do I convince my client or boss that we should prototype?

This is probably the toughest challenge faced by those who are new to prototyping. It's not that you don't want to, or that you're scared of trying and failing. It's that you can't seem to get your boss or client to see the value in prototyping.

The first chapter in this book focuses on the value of prototyping. In that chapter, you'll learn how to make the argument with your client or boss that you cannot afford *not* to prototype. In fact, *not* prototyping will cost you more in the end than the time and effort it takes to prototype. Additionally, I've included a number of case studies and insights throughout the book, which should give you additional ammunition to make the case for prototyping. See pages 5–9.

How do I get started?

You just jump in and do it. Don't feel like you have to learn a new tool such as Fireworks or how to code HTML. Instead, start with something simple—prototype with paper or PowerPoint. You can always work your way up to something more advanced. See Chapters 6–11.

TABLE OF CONTENTS

CHAPTER 4
Eight Guiding Principles   43

CHAPTER 5
Picking the Right Tool   57

CHAPTER 6
Paper and Other Analog Methods   65

FOREWORD

W hat's the difference between theory and practice? Albert Einstein once said, "In theory they are the same. In practice, they are not."

Practice makes perfect. Champion sports teams practice constantly. Zen masters will tell you that the only way to achieve enlightenment is practice. Practice is at the very root of learning. As you practice, you learn, and as you learn, you improve.

Prototyping is practice for people who design and make things. It's not simply another tool for your design toolkit—it's a design philosophy. When you prototype, you allow your design, product, or service to practice being itself. And as its maker, you learn more about your designs in this way than you ever could in any other way.

A prototype, quite simply, is different from other works of the imagination, because it's real. It exists independently, outside the mind. This means that it can be tested—you can imagine various scenarios that might try to break your model, and you can design experiments that test your hypothesis.

Without a prototype, you can't test your product until you have built it, and in today's volatile business environment, where new companies can dominate markets in a few short years—for example, Google started in 1998, Facebook in 2004, Twitter in 2007—to build a product or service before you test it is insane. It's like sending athletes onto the playing field without letting them practice beforehand. It's a recipe for failure.

So make prototypes and break them, test them and learn from them, model your ideas when they are still in their infancy, and continue to make and break them throughout the design process. Trial and error and continuous refinement—this is the way we learn as children and continue to learn as adults. And if it's good enough for us, shouldn't it be good enough for our design children, our ideas, and our imagination?

A book on prototyping can never be more than a prototype itself, a snapshot of a moment in time, since prototyping is a continuing process that never ends, any more than learning ends.

And let's not forget this: Prototyping is fun! It's a playful, social way to develop your ideas. It's in direct opposition to "design in a vacuum" or "design in an ivory tower." It's design with and for people. It's play. And play, like practice, is a learning activity. Play is a rehearsal for life.

But prototyping is more than practice and play. It's also a great leap for many people. It requires courage, passion, and commitment to do it well. You need to be fearless enough to look failure in the face and to listen when you want to defend yourself. Fearless enough to watch your design "baby" in the rough hands of strangers who don't understand what it is or what it is for. Fearless enough to calmly throw out weeks of work and try a new approach. Prototyping is parenting—a way of bringing new things into the world and helping them grow.

Todd Zaki Warfel has written a book steeped in practice and deep personal experience. He shares his design philosophy, the tools of his trade, and the best methods that he knows for making things work. You can trust him. He prototypes and practices constantly. He's fearless. He listens. He's playful. And, God help him, he's just become a parent twice over: not just of this book, but of a real biological prototype—a little boy named Elijah. So take a leap. Dive into this book. Try it, test it, break it. Prototype, practice, and play with the ideas yourself. Tell him what you love about it, where it's gone wrong, and how it can be improved. He will love you for it.

—Dave Gray
Founder and Chairman of Xplane

INTRODUCTION

Thisisthepart where I tell you why I decided to write a book on prototyping and why I wanted to write it for Rosenfeld Media. The truth is that it was one of three topics I was passionate about. I don't recall whether Lou initially approached me, or I approached him, but I do recall him saying something like, "A few people have been telling me I should talk to you about writing a book. Do you have something you'd like to write about?" And thus began the negotiation—I tried to sell Lou on a few subjects I was interested in, and he tried to sell me on writing for Rosenfeld Media.

Lou wasn't as excited about the other two topics as I had hoped, but he was excited about prototyping and that was enough. He also believed I could write the book on prototyping.

Rosenfeld Media (RM) was fairly new at the time. They weren't a publishing powerhouse (yet). I believed in what Lou was doing with RM—practitioner-focused, field-tested books. And as someone who runs a small design consultancy, a David in the sea of Goliaths, I was excited to support the little guy who was disrupting the field.

Why prototyping? Well, it was a timely subject. Turns out, there weren't any books on prototyping focused on designers or user-experience practitioners. There were books on prototyping for industrial design and software engineering, but not for people who were designing the interactions and experiences of software systems. The only book that came close was Carolyn Snyder's *Paper Prototyping: The Fast and Easy Way to Design and Refine User Interfaces.* It's a great book. I own it. But while I'm a huge paper prototyping advocate—it continues to be one of my favorite methods to teach—I felt our field needed something that covered multiple methods and tools.

Competition was practically nonexistent.

Prototyping was also something that had become a larger part of our practice at my design firm, Messagefirst. At the time, we were designing more and more transaction-based systems that leveraged AJAX-style interactions. We had pushed the limits of what we could do with wireframes and weren't getting the results we wanted. Wireframes were no longer effective for the kind of work we were doing. As good as our wireframe documentation model was, we were spending too much time explaining it. I don't like having to explain my work. If I have to explain it, it's broken.

Anyone who knows me knows that I'm continually looking for ways to evolve my craft, push my design process, and find solutions that are more efficient and effective. Our process was broken, and we needed to fix it. It was a design problem and I saw the solution—prototyping.

Prior to writing this book, my prototyping experience had been limited to paper, PowerPoint, Keynote, Flash, and HTML. I didn't want to write a book that was bigger than my personal experiences. This book isn't for me. This book is for you. So just like any design project, I decided to do a little research, which turned into nine months of research. I interviewed dozens of practitioners, ran a few surveys, played with more prototyping tools than I can remember, and then took a deep breath.

One of my first realizations was that I was going to have to learn to prototype with some new tools. I had used Visio and Fireworks before, but not to prototype. I had never used Axure RP Pro.

I learned and experienced a lot in writing this book. I learned new methods and tools. I learned a number of tips and techniques from fellow practitioners. I learned about prototyping successes and failures from fellow practitioners, and even experienced a number of successes and failures of my own.

I wrote this book so you can learn how prototyping will change your design process. I wrote this book to share my experiences and the experiences of others, to show you the value of prototyping, and to give you the tools you'll need to convince your boss or client that you can't afford *not* to prototype on your next project.

CHAPTER 1

The Value of Prototyping

E very year, millions of people get a glimpse into the future—the concept car. Manufacturers invest several years and millions of dollars into these one-of-a-kind creations. Most of them never make it to mass production. Those that do are often a fraction of the original vision.

The automotive industry is highly competitive. Innovation is not only a means to stay ahead, but also often one of survival. Each concept is an exercise in design, an exploration into what's possible, what's feasible, and what's marketable—it's a *prototype*.

This method of prototyping has been a core part of the auto industry for decades. While these concept cars are expensive, it's much more expensive to retool all the necessary machines and launch a failure. The risk is too high.

Making the argument that prototyping is a necessary part of the overall design process for something like a car or a missile guidance system is a no-brainer. However, in the world of software development, the argument for gaining buy-in for creating a prototype is a bit more challenging. In fact, it's typically one of the greatest challenges we have.

In this first chapter, I'm going to highlight some of the challenges faced when trying to incorporate prototyping into an existing design/development process. I'm also going to give you a few pointers to show how valuable prototyping can be to identify problems early on, reduce risk, and ultimately save time, effort, and money.

Clients and management who aren't familiar with prototyping often see it as a cost with little, if any, benefit. It's one of the most common questions I've received, "How do I get my boss or client to buy into prototyping? They say we don't have the time or budget for it."

If your business is involved in building Web sites, software applications, or systems that have both a hardware and software component, you can't afford *not* to prototype. As the complexity of the system increases, the cost-to-benefit ratio of prototyping increases dramatically.

Prototyping does have a cost. It isn't free. But if you haven't been proto-typing, you've been missing opportunities for innovation and significant cost savings. The benefits of prototyping far outweigh the initial cost.

Prototyping Is Generative

One of the fundamental values of prototyping is that it's generative, which means as you work through the prototyping process, you're going to generate hundreds, if not thousands, of ideas. Some of them are brilliant and some are less brilliant. I've found that even those less brilliant ideas can be a catalyst for brilliant solutions.

As a generative process, prototyping often leads to innovation and a significant savings in time, effort, and cost. Prototyping helps you get ideas out of your head and into something more tangible—something you can feel, experience, work through, play with, and test.

Prototyping—The Power of Show, Tell, and Experience

If a picture is worth a thousand words, then a prototype is worth 10,000. Prototypes go beyond the power of show and tell—they let you experience the design.

> *"It's one thing to talk about them and have storyboards and an-other thing to see them for real."*
>
> —Robert Hoekman, Jr.

There are a number of ways to communicate or document a design, including requirements documents, wireframes, visual comps, and prototypes.

Common Design Documentation Models

Requirements documents. These are typically a written document describing the technical or functional requirements of a system.

Requirements documents tend to be more focused on written description and less on visual illustration—they are more *tell* and less *show*. The lack of visual simulation often leads to misinterpretation of a requirement. Screen shots can be included to help reduce this misinterpretation, but static screens only go so far.

Wireframes. Ever seen architectural blueprints for a house? Well, that's kind of what a wireframe is for software. Wireframes are a visual representation of the functional page structure. They visually communicate what functional pieces are present on a page and their relationship to each other. Wireframes are typically in black and white or shades of gray.

Combined with detailed behavior notes, wireframes do a better job at show and tell than requirements. However, wireframes often leave gaps in the design. These gaps result in missing details or misinterpretation, which is bad.

Prototypes. A prototype is a representative model or simulation of the final system. Unlike requirements documents and wireframes, prototypes go further than show and tell and actually let you experience the design.

Some technical requirements, like a 100KB page limit, might not be obvious in a prototype. These can easily be captured with a supplemental document much smaller than 60–200 pages.

On its own, a requirements document or wireframe is insufficient for show and tell of complex systems. You might be able to get by using one of these for simple systems, but for complex systems, you'll ultimately run into trouble. Oftentimes, they are used together in the attempt to create a "full picture." However, they still fall short when it comes to actually experiencing the design.

Combining annotated wireframes with a requirements document can get you to a 70–80 percent accuracy of the original vision. That's still too much room for error in my book.

The AJAX and RIA Monkey Wrench

Now, what happens if you throw AJAX or other Rich Internet Applications (RIAs) into the mix? Things start to fall apart—rapidly. Neither a requirements document nor annotated wireframes do a good job at telling the story of rich interactions and transitions.

Unlike traditional page-based interactions, AJAX and RIAs often leverage state-based interactions. A page or screen can have several tiles or widgets that operate independently and interdependently of each other. Updating an RSS feed on a page doesn't require refreshing the entire page anymore. Instead, only the RSS feed widget updates, leaving the rest of the page alone.

This has prompted many in the design community to claim that the page paradigm is dead—the new paradigm is the screen or state.

Transitions and animations are another challenge. Have you ever tried to describe a self-healing AJAX transition? My best description, coupled with some strategic hand waving and magic wand simulations, still results in raised eyebrows and questionable looks.

As the presence of AJAX and other RIA technologies continue to grow, the need for and value of prototypes as a design communication tool dramatically increases. In fact, I would argue it becomes critical for success.

Prototyping Reduces Misinterpretation

Take a 60-page requirements document. Bring 15 people into a room. Hand it out. Let them all read it. Now ask them what you're building. You're going to get 15 different answers. Imagine trying the same thing with a 200-page requirements document—it gets even worse.

Prototypes are a more concrete and tactile representation of the system you're building. They provide tangible experiences.

Once my company made a shift away from a requirements-dependent process to a prototype-dependent process, we saw an immediate reduction in the need for clarification and rework. We've gone from a 60–80 percent consensus on interpretation to 90 percent or better.

We've also found that the total amount of time and effort required to produce the prototype is less than that required to create a detailed specification document and annotated wireframes.

I've found a number of reasons that written documentation leaves more room for misinterpretation:

- Nobody wants to read a 60–200-page written specification. There's really no joy in it.

- If you can't get them to read it, you won't get them to fully understand it.

- Written documentation doesn't allow you to see the "big picture." Instead, you're forced to see one line at a time.

- Words leave too much room for interpretation.

Prototypes, on the other hand, have a number of advantages that help reduce misinterpretation:

- You experience how the system would work, rather than just read about it.

- Prototypes encourage play. When you get someone to play with your prototype, you increase the likelihood that they'll understand it.

Prototyping Saves Time, Effort, and Money

How many times have you heard one of the following from a client, one of your bosses, or even a fellow designer or developer?

"We don't have time to prototype."

"We can't afford to prototype. We don't have the budget for it."

I've heard each of these arguments dozens of times. Frankly, they're not without some merit. As I said earlier, prototyping isn't free, but the benefits of prototyping far outweigh the cost of prototyping, or most importantly, *not* prototyping.

Talk to anyone who has made the transition from a design and development process that didn't include prototyping to one that does, and they'll tell you it has saved them a ton of time and headaches. Not only does prototyping let you realize and experience the design faster, but ultimately it also reduces the amount of waste created by other design and development processes.

Prototyping Reduces Waste

In a typical design and development process, requirements are written and handed off to a designer or developer. The designer or developer then interprets these requirements and builds something based on his/her interpretation.

Theoretically, a requirements-driven design process should reduce waste. The overall goal is to get everyone on the same page. If we're all on the same page, ultimately, we'll have less waste. Sounds fantastic.

Theoretically, it's a very sound idea. As experience will show, however, theory and reality are often very different. There are a number of shortcomings in a traditional requirements-driven design and development process that create waste, and they include the following:

1. **Written by the wrong person.** Designers and developers are rarely included in the requirements writing process. Instead, the requirements are often written by a business analyst or his equivalent. This person lacks the technical and design knowledge of their counterparts, which often results in any number of requirements being rewritten several times.

2. **Significant time and effort.** The amount of time invested in writing, reviewing, and revising these detailed requirements is significant. For complex systems, I've seen it take 3–9 months to finish something— sometimes more. During that time, things change.

3. **Non-final final.** Theoretically, the requirements are the final documentation. In reality, requirements are constantly changing, even after they're "complete."

4. **Misinterpretation.** The amount of misinterpretation of the 60–200-page requirements is often significant. Misinterpretation leads to weeks or months of rework and a delayed product launch.

5. **Nonessential features.** Requirements are often filled with features that provide little, if any, value. Those features take time and effort to build and test. This results in wasted time in writing requirements, building, and testing features that provide little, if any, value and often go unused.

6. **Catching mistakes too late.** Requirements-driven processes typically won't catch a mistake until it's in production. The later you catch a mistake in the development process, the more costly it is to fix.

Any one of these items alone creates wasted time and effort. Typically, a requirements-driven process is plagued with several of these issues, creating a great deal of inefficiency and waste. On the other hand, including prototyping in the process can help reduce the amount of waste and result in these benefits:

1. **Decisions by the right people.** Designers and developers can flex their experience and knowledge, contribute to the process, and ultimately ensure that the right people make the design decisions.

2. **Survival of the fittest.** Multiple ideas are created and tested to ensure that the strongest solutions survive.

3. **Adaptive.** Prototypes can be quickly updated, compensating for the ever-changing nature of software development.

4. **Reduced misinterpretation.** The prototype is a visual, or sometimes physical, representation of the system. Visual and physical representations leave less room for misinterpretation than a 60–200-page written document. By reducing misinterpretation, you reduce the amount of rework. Less rework means lower costs and faster time to market.

5. **Focus.** Prototyping produces more focused products. More focused products produce less waste in design, development, and rework.

6. **Catch mistakes early.** Prototyping helps you catch mistakes early in the design and development process. The earlier you catch a mistake, the lower the cost to fix it will be.

7. **Reduce risk.** Prototyping reduces risk, by reducing misinterpretation and catching problems earlier in the design and development cycle.

While prototyping can't solve all the problems that plague requirements-driven processes, it can definitely help reduce many of the more common inefficiencies and waste.

Prototyping Provides Real-World Value

Jonathan Baker-Bates is someone who has seen a measurable benefit from prototyping firsthand. Jonathan works for a consulting company in the UK with a very typical design and development story. His team of developers regularly receives a 200-page specification document to quote against and build to. Well, that was what they used to do.

Jonathan's company recently made a shift toward a prototyping-oriented process. Instead of giving developers a 200-page document, they now receive a high-fidelity prototype with a 16-page supporting document.

Since the change, his company has noticed a number of significant improvements:

- Time and effort required to produce the prototype and 16-page supplemental document is less than half required for the 200-page specification document.

- Estimates for build time and cost have become 50 percent more accurate.

- Request for clarification by the development team has been reduced by 80 percent.

- The amount of rework and bug fixes post-launch has been reduced to 25 percent of similar previous projects.

- All team members agree that executing the design with the prototyping process is easier than the old process.

Case Study: Prototyping with Tight Budgets and Deadlines

by Jonathan Baker-Bates

With less than four months to design and build a "social" Web site for a major computer games developer, we had a strong visual design concept, a number of broad content and functionality requirements, and a team of in-house developers ready to go with a CMS. But budgets were tight, and there were plenty of uncertainties about the scope of the project. This was also the first time we had worked with this particular client, and they were not the sort who were given to studying large documents (which could often top 200 pages on similar projects). We needed to keep everyone engaged and clear about what we intended to do from the earliest stages.

We decided that from day one of the design phase, all eyes were to be on a functional HTML prototype, which demonstrated the entire site, built and maintained using Axure. With that in mind, we hoped to show almost all the necessary requirements to a level of detail for anyone and everyone to grasp—whether they were a CEO or a CMS integrator.

Of course, the prototype could not show everything. Nonfunctional elements, some conditional screens, and exceptional flows needed to be recorded separately, as well as miscellaneous notes about the implementation. These were captured in a short supporting document of around 20 pages. The one rule that applied to this document was that it would contain only those things that could not reasonably be understood from the prototype. This was important to minimize our overhead and prevent the document from running out of control.

Case Study: Prototyping with Tight Budgets and Deadlines (continued)

The first thing we noticed was that the prototype removed the need for lengthy "introductory" communication and discussion. People who viewed the prototype became immediately familiar with what we were trying to do in minutes rather than hours or days. That meant that we could turn the discussion back to the details. This rewarded us in a number of ways. First, the accuracy of the build estimates proved to be very high. Second, we also encountered a far lower amount of communication (and problems) about the design overall—perhaps as much as 80 percent less than normal. Finally, when the design later went to integration and testing, it had a relatively smooth passage with about 25 percent fewer bugs being reported against the specification. Budgetary and scope constraints still meant that things were often difficult, but having a prototype meant that we could quickly show how we intended to scale back some requirements to get the client's sign-off.

For us, this approach proved successful. However, I'd caution readers to remember that all projects are different, and this technique might not have been best in other circumstances. It is also worth noting that we later returned to a more traditional document-based process for incremental changes once the main site had gone live. But without the prototype on hand, we would probably not have been able to deliver when we did.

Jonathan's story isn't anything unique. It's the same story told by people I interviewed for this book. I've heard similar stories from dozens of people who have attended one of my prototyping workshops or talks. And it's been reiterated again by hundreds of respondents to surveys I conducted while writing this book.

Summary

Prototyping can literally shave months to years off your development time. What are you waiting for?

Now that you know the value of prototyping, you should be able to get buy-in from clients or management. Just remember the following key points:

- Prototyping is generative.
- Prototypes communicate through show and tell.
- Prototyping reduces misinterpretation.
- Prototyping saves time, effort, and money.
- Prototyping creates a rapid feedback loop, which ultimately reduces risk.

In the next chapter, we're going to look at the rapid, iterative prototyping process I use.

The Prototyping Process

In architecture and product design, prototyping is a given. But that's not necessarily the case with software development.

—Anders Ramsay

P rototyping is commonplace in other design fields like architecture and industrial design. In fact, it's not just accepted, but expected.

Why isn't it as expected in software development? After all, software development, architecture, and industrial design have so much in common, including the following characteristics:

- They are all design processes.

- Artifacts are produced to communicate the design.

- The end result is a tangible product that people can experience and use.

I think the first reason is that in software development, the emphasis is often placed on the development process and not the design process. The industry doesn't call it "software design"; they call it "software development."

In software development, design is often an afterthought. The emphasis is on the technology or features—not the design. In architecture and industrial design, however, the emphasis is on design. Form follows function.

Another reason is that software development is seen as a manufacturing process, but architecture and industrial design are seen as a craft.

Perhaps these shortcomings are the result of how each field is taught. Computer science classes focus on teaching students technologies. Architecture and industrial design, on the other hand, focus on teaching students design principles and include something called *design studio*.

The Absence of Design Studio

In the world of architecture and industrial design, a design studio is a process, not just a physical place. This process is taught in every respectable architecture and industrial design program. You'll be hard pressed to find a design studio class in computer science.

In studio classes, you design or prototype and present to your peers. Your peers critique your work, highlighting the strengths and areas that still need some work.

When you design, present, and critique, think of it as a collaborative, rapid, iterative design process. During this process, you get to share in the ideas, successes, and failures of your peers.

Design studio is a core part of architecture and industrial design. Prototyping is a core part of that studio process. So students learn this skill early on, and they use it regularly. Prototyping becomes a regular tool in their design process.

What Does the Prototyping Process Look Like?

First, let's be clear about something—there is no uber-prototyping process, a single formula like there is for Coca-Cola. However, there are a number of tried-and-true guiding principles you can follow, no matter what you're prototyping.

Second, no matter what prototyping process you decide to use, keep in mind that a *process* is merely a means to an end. One of the most common pitfalls of following a process is being tied too tightly to it. If you're more focused on the process than the end goal, you won't be successful.

Third, a good process balances structure with flexibility. It provides a solid foundation, while giving you the flexibility to change and adapt that process as needed, due to changes in time or circumstance.

Finally, a good process breeds success. When your process starts to limit success, then you need to revisit it.

Mark Sanders, the inventor of the Strida folding bicycles, describes the process he used to create the bikes on YouTube[1]. As I watched Mark describe his process, a few things stood out:

- He didn't worry about which ideas were good and which were bad. Instead, he used sketching to explore every possible idea.

---

1 toddwarfel.com/archives/great-video-on-prototyping-bikes/

- Once he had plenty of sketches, he evaluated them based on the original goals of the product. This left him with the best ideas.

- Sketches only go so far. In order to see which of his best ideas would really work, he had to build models or prototypes.

- Sketching also played a critical part in updating the design to create the Strida2.

The process Mark describes in the video is a pretty typical prototyping process, which includes the following elements:

- Sketching

- Evaluation

- Modeling

- Testing

At my company, Messagefirst, we use a similar approach to the one Mark describes, but with a small twist. Our prototyping process takes a page from the design studio book and uses the presentation and critique model for evaluation. So our modified approach looks like this:

- Sketching (e.g., whiteboards, paper, code)

- Presentation and critique

- Modeling (prototyping)

- Testing

Since one of the goals of our process is rapid iteration and evolution, we stress some pretty short timeframes on the first two stages—sketching and presentation and critique. This emphasis on short cycles keeps the process moving and makes us more productive. It also enhances the generative nature of prototyping.

Our prototyping process is also *iterative and evolutionary*. We sketch, present and critique, prototype, present and critique, sketch, present and critique, prototype, present and critique, prototype, and test (see Figure 2.1). Then we do it all again.

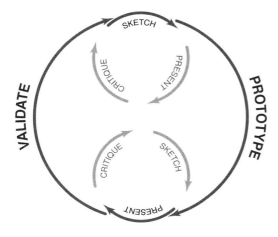

FIGURE 2.1
Diagram of the iterative design and critique process.

One thing you might have noticed is the cyclical nature and multiple instances of the first two steps: sketching and presentation and critique. Sketching is woven throughout our prototyping process. Anytime we sketch, we present and critique. In fact, when we're presenting and critiquing our prototypes, either internally or externally with a client, we sketch our revisions.

Now, let's take a detailed look at the prototyping process I use, starting with sketching.

Part 1: Sketching

Sketching is the generative part of prototyping. As part of the generative nature of prototyping, your goal is to get the ideas out of your head and into a more tangible format.

I prefer putting a time limit on "sketching time." This forces the sketchers to work quickly without getting caught up in the details.

The goal of sketching isn't to flesh out your ideas fully—you'll do that during the prototyping stage of the process. The goal is to generate a number of concepts, get them out of your head as quickly as possible, and move on.

> ### TIP QUANTITY OVER QUALITY
>
> When you're sketching, don't worry about good ideas versus bad ideas. The purpose of sketching is to explore ideas. Sketching is where quantity is more important that quality. Quality will come later.

Sketches are typically rough, somewhat incomplete, and frankly, sketchy, like Figure 2.2. Don't be concerned about making them perfect. Just get the ideas out of your head and make them tangible.

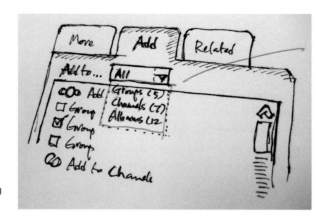

FIGURE 2.2
Sketch of Vimeo video browser module showing line weight and labels.[2]

> ### TIP FAST AND FURIOUS
>
> Put a time limit on your sketching. I like to do limits of 10–30 minutes and then move on to the presentation and critique stage. These short time limits force you to focus more on producing ideas than getting caught up in the details.

Most of our sketching is done on paper using sketchboards. Sketchboards are just a piece of paper with a bunch of miniature windows for sketching. Sketchboards look like storyboards.

Here's an example of what one of our sketchboards looks like (see in Figure 2.3).

---

2 www.flickr.com/photos/soxiam/2532060829/

CHAPTER 2

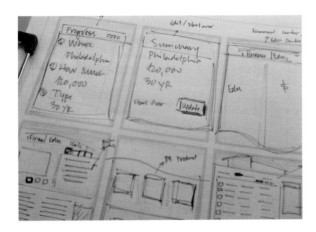

FIGURE 2.3
Sketchboard example
showing multiple sketches.

The biggest difference between a storyboard and a sketchboard is that storyboards are used to tell a linear story. Sketchboards, on the other hand, are just intended to capture a bunch of ideas—linear, nonlinear, it really doesn't matter.

TIP   GOOD THINGS COME IN SMALL PACKAGES

Using sketchboards is a great way to generate several ideas. The small space encourages you to think about specific parts of the interface. Sketchboards are also flexible enough to be used for a little storyboarding if you need to describe AJAX or RIA designs.

While most of our sketching is done on paper, we will occasionally sketch on whiteboards or in code. Sketch in whatever medium you're comfortable in as long as it produces results.

Let's have a quick look at some of the advantages and disadvantages of sketching in code, on a whiteboard, or on paper.

Sketching in Code

Sketching is limited to paper or a whiteboard. Developers often sketch in their medium, which is source code. Just like sketching with paper or a whiteboard, you sketch out your ideas by constructing them with bits of source code.

One of the benefits of sketching with code is the inherent ease of turning your sketches into a prototype. With the increasing number of JavaScript libraries, CSS frameworks, and application frameworks like Ruby on Rails, sketching in code is easier than ever.

Advantages

- It makes sketching in code easier with an increasing number of available tools.

- It brings your sketches to life—you can actually play with your sketches.

- It leverages existing code, when possible.

Disadvantages

- Not everyone can code.

- It requires a computer.

- It's less collaborative than paper or a whiteboard.

- It takes more time than paper or a whiteboard.

Sketching on Whiteboards

One of the biggest benefits of sketching on whiteboards is its inherent collaborative nature. It's very easy for anyone to participate in the discussion and sketch on the whiteboard.

Advantages

- It's collaborative.

- Anyone can draw on a whiteboard.

- More than one person can participate at a time.

- No computer is necessary.

- Revisions are easy—just erase and draw again.

Disadvantages

- It's less portable than code or paper.

- Sketches are still static.

- Capturing sketches from a whiteboard can be difficult.[1]

Sketching on Paper

Sketching on paper is still my favorite. Similar to the collaborative nature of sketching on whiteboards, paper is ultra portable and can be done anywhere.

Advantages

- It's collaborative.

- Anyone can draw on paper.

- More than one person can participate at a time.

- No computer is necessary.

- Revisions are easy—just draw over your current sketch or grab another piece of paper.

- It can happen anytime, anywhere.

- It's definitely portable.

Disadvantages

- Sketches are still static.

Part 2: Presentation and Critique

Presentation and critique is arguably the most important part of our prototyping process. This is where we focus on quality.

Presentation and critique is a technique I learned from studio class during my undergraduate days while studying graphic design. And even though

---

3   Sketches can be captured with photos or using a Smartboard.

I later changed my degree to English and Cognitive Psychology, I'll never forget the very valuable lessons learned from presentation and critique.

The goal of the presentation and critique stage is to find the best ideas. You present the strengths of your concept, and your peers highlight areas that need work or further clarification. That's it—discuss, evaluate, and move on.

When presenting our sketches for critique, we often taped them up on a wall, as shown in Figure 2.4.

FIGURE 2.4
Presentation of sketches during a design studio critique session.

Presentation and Critique Guidelines

Keep it short. As I mentioned earlier, presentation and critique is the second stage where we emphasize tight timelines. In fact, presentation and critique time is shorter than sketching time. I like to limit presentation time to two minutes and critique to three minutes.

It's important not to spend too much time during the presentation and critique step. I know, it sounds a bit counterintuitive. But just like when you're sketching, the purpose is to get something out quickly and move on. You're going to refine your ideas later.

Three-minute presentation per concept. A time limit of three minutes per presentation per concept means that you'll have to focus on the strongest parts. And if you can't explain your concept in less than two minutes, then something is probably wrong with it.

Two-minute critique. Your peers get two minutes to critique your concept. During the critique, they have to provide two to three things they think are strong about it and one to two areas that need improvement or need to be worked out a bit more.

Take notes. Write directly on your prototype sketches. It's okay. It's just paper. Use the critique of your peers to refine and strengthen your design concept.

Part 3: Prototype

At this point in the process, you've sketched out your ideas, presented and had them critiqued, and are now left with the strongest concepts. These are the ones you're going to prototype.

Prototyping is where you start to work out the details of your design and figure out which ones will actually work.

When I prototype, I consider the following details:

- Am I using a tool or medium I'm comfortable in?

- Do I have the ability to communicate effectively what I need to the *audience* or *consumer*?

- How much time do I have?

- What level of fidelity do I need?

It really doesn't matter what you build your prototype in at this stage. Most of my prototypes are HTML/AJAX prototypes, but that's due to the nature of my work and clients. I've also created Flash, Keynote, and paper prototypes.

Once I have a prototype, I repeat the presentation and critique stage. I use the same basic model, presenting a piece of the prototype at a time and offering it up for critique from the client or customer. The biggest difference is when I present a prototype, I increase the time limits on presentation and critique. Other than that, the process follows the same guidelines.

> **TIP PROJECT AND SKETCH**
>
> Project your prototype on a whiteboard during the presentation and critique process. This allows you to sketch on top of your prototype during the process.

Part 4: Test

I divide testing into one of two categories: testing with the client or testing with the end consumer.

Testing with Clients

Testing with the client is a hybrid model of presentation and critique with sketching. These sessions typically last 1.5–3 hours, depending on the complexity of the prototype.

During these sessions, I follow the basic presentation and critique model, presenting one piece at a time and opening it up for discussion. Rather than writing up a list of revisions, I use a sketchboard to create sketch notes. These sketch notes are mostly sketches with a few labels or handwritten notes added.

I've found that sketching out the revisions ensures that we all walk away from the table on the same page. Written notes leave too much room for misinterpretation. By sketching the revisions, the risk of misinterpretation is reduced. And since sketching is collaborative, the client can contribute easily to the solution.

Basically, I follow the prototyping process for defining revisions during the prototype process—more sketching, less writing.

Once the design review session is finished, the client gets access to a copy of the prototype, and I ask him to play with it for the next two to three days.

Since one of the goals of a prototype is to get it into the audience's hands, I want the client to experience it, play with it, and use it. After he does, he'll either find additional issues, or realize that something he thought was an issue really isn't.

Testing with End Customers

Testing with the end customer is a standard usability test—8–12 participants, 5–6 scenarios, audio-video capture, analysis, and reporting of results afterward. Check out Chapter 12, "Testing Your Prototype," for more detailed information on testing your prototype.

In either case, client or customer testing, I incorporate the feedback into the next iteration of the prototype.

Summary

So that's an overview of the prototyping process I use at Messagefirst. Hopefully, this has helped newbies see how prototyping can improve their design process. And for those seasoned pros, I hope you found a few tips to improve your current prototyping process.

Prototyping is a process, not a product—like any other process, it's only a means to an end. A few important points to remember when you're prototyping:

- Sketching is a key part of the prototyping process.

- Use the design studio method of sketching, presenting, and critiquing as a way to iterate rapidly.

- Start with quantity, exploring lots of ideas. Quality will come later.

In the next two chapters, we'll look at the five different types of prototypes and the eight guiding principles for better prototyping.

CHAPTER 3

Five Types of Prototypes

Before beginning this book, I knew there would be a number of different types of prototypes—anyone with a measurable amount of prototyping under his or her belt knows that. While I cannot say that I discovered a new type of prototype or purpose for prototypes, I can say that discussions with other practitioners led me to a new way of thinking about prototyping.

During my frequent discussions with practitioners and vendors, the usual suspects for types of prototypes surfaced repeatedly—for example, they are a way of communicating a concept or idea, a way to sell your idea internally, a way to market your idea to customers, and a way to determine what's feasible.

However, it was a discussion with user experience designer Jed Wood that brought out one of those "ah-hah" moments. Jed shone some light on something that had been sitting there all along—*prototyping as a way to work through your own designs.*

Like I said, it wasn't as if I had suddenly discovered a new type of prototype. In fact, it was during our conversation that I realized I had been doing this all along. I just never thought of it this way until my discussion with Jed. As a practitioner, this is probably the most valuable reason to prototype.

Type 1: Shared Communication

Having a common communication platform reduces that misinterpretation I wrote about earlier. Prototypes act as a common visual language for communication. In any given project, you may have a number of different parties who share a common directive, namely to get a product out the door, keep the company alive, and get paid for another day at work. But let's not forget, they also have their own language and agenda.

Ever been in the same room with a group of engineers and marketing people? They can't talk to each other. Well, they can talk, but they can't really have a conversation. They don't understand each other. They speak two different languages. Throw a visual designer, information architect, and usability specialist into the mix and whoo-hah, grab the popcorn and soda, boys and girls, and sit back and enjoy the show.

So what do you do? Get some paper or a whiteboard and have a quick-and-dirty collaborative prototyping session. Grab a designer and a developer and sketch out the ideas together. They don't have to be perfect or beautiful, they just need to communicate the intent of the ideas behind the design. Do it together. Collaborate. Sketch.

Using prototyping as a collaborative tool has a number of benefits. First, it opens the lines of communication between the two groups. Second, it provides an opportunity for the groups to learn to communicate with one another. But most importantly, getting designers and developers to work together to collectively flesh out the ideas *builds* relationships.

When designers and developers have a relationship with each other, good things happen. Designers are more likely to get developers to try something new, to push their own boundaries, to bend a current technology to do something it wasn't meant to do, to work around a constraint, or to invent a new technology—necessity *is* the mother of invention. Designers can push developers to find out what they actually *can* and *cannot* do.

Developers can provide insights into the technology, giving designers access to capabilities they never knew existed. But they can also act as a checkpoint, a way of helping the designers keep one foot on the shore so they don't go too far out to sea and sink the ship in some turbulent storm. Developers can help designers see what is reasonable and feasible.

> **TIP PLAYS WELL WITH OTHERS**
>
> Collaborative prototyping is a great team-building exercise. Consider this approach. Get some designers and developers in a room together and have them prototype as a relationship-building exercise. Its common communication platform becomes an immediate benefit. As a hidden benefit, putting the two groups together can help designers see what's reasonable and developers will see what they actually *can* or *cannot* do.

Another major benefit of prototypes as a communication platform comes into play with geographically distributed teams. As companies grow, their teams become segmented. Marketing is on one floor, design on another, and development still on another. Grow even bigger, and your teams might be in different buildings. Bigger still, your teams are in different cities. And let's not forget offshore businesses, where your development team is in India, Russia, or China.

In these situations, communication can be a challenge. And in today's world, much of the communication takes place over conference calls, instant messenger, or email—even if you are in the same building. If your company is based in California and your development team is in Eastern Europe or Asia, then you can also run into time zone and possible language issues. These potential problems can all be solved with a prototype, which is a common communication language.

Prototypes help remove the language barrier by acting as a common communication platform to *show* instead of *tell*. Prototypes are also time-zone independent. You can spend more time *showing* the development team how you want the product to function and less time attempting to *tell* them. The reverse is also true—the development team can build a prototype to show you how they understand you want the product to function.

One method for showing and telling is something Robert Hoekman, Jr. refers to as protocasting. Similar to podcasting and screen casting, Hoekman creates a series of screens, typically using OmniGraffle, and records the simulation as he walks through critical parts of the prototype.

Protocommunicating

by Robert Hoekman, Jr.

(www.rhjr.net, www.miskeeto.com)

There's no doubt that a prototype can speak volumes about the design of an interaction or even an entire application. But prototyping has benefits far beyond that of fleshing out a complete idea to show stakeholders how an application will work or to scope out the technical feasibility of a project.

Protocommunicating (continued)

Ultimately, a prototype is a communication tool. It can certainly be used for marketing purposes or to close the communication gap across multiple project teams, but prototypes can also readily be used in much more micro-level ways—to communicate much smaller ideas, when words or static images simply won't cut it. As such, and with the right tools, they can be used often and can become an integral part of your design process.

Let me put this in context.

When working on rich interfaces, such as for an RIA or a Web 2.0-style, "on-demand" interface, it can be difficult to detail the multiple states of a single screen, or a single interaction within a screen, through individual images. To break these interactions into digestible pieces, I usually create a storyboard—a series of wireframes showing the screen states in the order the interaction occurs. And, of course, I do my best to document these interactions using detailed use cases in a Design Description Document (**www.rhjr.net/ddd**). But often, this simply isn't enough.

There are two problems with storyboards. First, they require me to visualize the shift from one state to the next without being able to click my way through it firsthand. Second, it forces clients to do the same thing. While storyboards do work well for many interactions, prototypes can bring an idea to life and force everyone to examine the designs in a way that could not have been done with static images alone, even in storyboard format.

Now, I use OmniGraffle quite a bit for interaction design work, and it supports the assignment of some basic click actions to wireframes and diagrams. This means I can quickly create and export a very basic, lo-res, click-through prototype as a PDF document any time I need it.

In doing this, not only can I deliver a document everyone is able to open and play around with, but I also can take things a step further by recording a video narrative of the prototype using a tool such as Snapz Pro X (Mac) or Camtasia (Windows).

Protocommunicating (continued)

These "protocasts" (www.rhjr.net/shorty/protocasting), as I call them, are simply screen recordings of my interaction with the prototype, accompanied by some running audio commentary about the interaction as I go through it. This can include thoughts on technical constraints, areas of the design that may need further improvement, and so on.

Protocasts have been fantastic not only for explaining interactions in more depth than I can do with storyboards, but also when doing usability reviews and other critiques. I simply record my screen as I complete a task in an application, and narrate my critiques as I go along. I can even do this from a hypothetical user's point-of-view, saying things like, "I don't really understand what this label means [...]. Maybe I'll just click this other button instead and see what happens [...]. Oops—that's not what I wanted."

Because it takes extremely little effort to create a PDF prototype with OmniGraffle and follow it up with a protocast, there is almost no cost in time or energy to do so. As a result, I've been able to do this often and make it a fairly regular part of my workflow. And the little time it does take to create these artifacts is more than made up for by the time saved in question-and-answer sessions, which invariably result from a wireframe-only deliverable.

Instead of spending a lot of time on a complicated, feature-rich prototype of a full application, I create prototypes and protocasts only for the interactions that really need the most explanation. These deliverables are usually very small in scope, typically documenting only a single screen or interaction, so they take very little time to create while still offering all the benefits of prototyping.

All in all, it's a cheap, fast, and painless solution that has helped me communicate ideas and critiques on many occasions when words simply weren't enough and a full-fledged prototype would be overkill.

Good communication is an essential element of a successful design project. Using prototypes and protocasts, everyone can stay on the same page with very little cost or effort.

Type 2: Working Through a Design

In the world of redesign, there are two models: the day at the spa and the extreme makeover.

The day at the spa is the same face, just a little fresher. Maybe you add a few new features, make a few enhancements, fix a few things, but overall, it's still the same animal. It's really more of a realign than a redesign.

The extreme makeover, however, is an entirely different animal. You're breaking new boundaries, trying radically new ideas, new design concepts. You've got a new face, shed a few pounds, model your new wardrobe—your friends might not even recognize you anymore. This can either be really good or a complete disaster.

Before launching an extreme makeover, you need to test it. You need a way to explore these different designs, work your way through them, test them, and refine them. Prototypes are a great way to actually work through the designs, test them out, see which ones will work, and flesh out the details.

Type 3: Selling Your Idea Internally

In most cases, doing the right thing for your customers and providing a better user experience will ultimately benefit your bottom line. In fact, to test this idea, a UX consulting firm, Teehan+Lax, set up a UX fund investing in companies focused on providing superior experiences to see how they performed against the rest of the industry.

As of November 2007, their UX Fund was up 39.5 percent.[1] That's an impressive number in itself. It's even more impressive when you consider that the market wasn't doing so well in November 2007. Ultimately, investing in a better UX is in a business's best interest, but that can take some convincing.

A few years ago, I had the opportunity to work on one of the first commercially available Voice Over IP (VoIP) products on the market. This was actually my second stab at a VoIP product—the first fell victim to the dot-com bomb.

---

[1] www.teehanlax.com/blog/?p=293

When finding solutions for an interaction problem, looking at the competition is a common method. Another method is to look at parallel products (for example, mobile phones, office phones, home phones). Yet another method, my favorite, in fact, is to simply explore new interaction models and solutions. Since every problem has multiple solutions, selecting the best solution can be tricky.

Let's look at one of the features that was in this VoIP product, which is common in just about any phone—speed dial. Traditional phone devices allow you to add one speed dial number at a time. Much of this is due to the limited screen real estate on a typical phone, be it home, mobile, or office. On a computer, however, you have more screen real estate to work with, and therefore your options increase.

There are traditional methods for allowing someone to store multiple numbers or pieces of data on the Web—just give them dozens of input boxes on the screen. It does technically accomplish the goal, but having dozens of input fields for phone numbers on a screen isn't exactly my idea of a clean design. So I came up with a different concept, which was a method to dynamically add more fields on demand. Start with a clean design and build on it as needed.

I described my idea to the product manager and engineering team and then showed them a sketch similar to Figure 3.1. Upon seeing the sketch, they started to understand the concept. Management loved the idea, but engineering wanted to stick with a bunch of static fields because it would be easier to implement. (In the next section, you'll see what eventually happened to my idea.)

Much like selling your idea internally, prototypes work as a tool to sell the technical feasibility and value of your concept. In some cases, your prototype can be so effective that senior management will tell engineering to just figure out how to build it.

TIP SHOWING IS BETTER THAN TELLING

Don't just talk about the ideas, show the different design solutions. Create a quick prototype of the different design solutions that are possible. Put them in front of the other team members and get their feedback. That way, you can use the prototype as a tool to make design decisions.

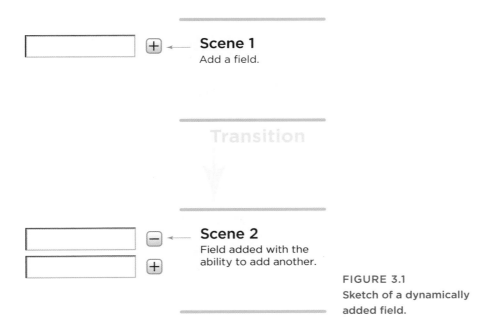

FIGURE 3.1
Sketch of a dynamically added field.

Type 4: Usability Testing

Remember the VoIP app I just discussed? One of the things we needed was buy-in from engineering. Since they weren't convinced, we decided to do some usability testing. This would give us real data to show whether or not our concept was solid. If it worked, great. We'd be able to take the data to management and engineering and have a strong argument. If not, then we'd know quickly and pursue another design.

Prior to testing, I was confident that people would get the dynamic input field model, but I wasn't convinced that it would be instinctively intuitive. I expected we'd have a few participants who got it and several who didn't get it immediately, but would learn it with subsequent use.

> A wireframe doesn't get that "Hey, that's really cool" effect. I've never received that from a set of wireframes.
>
> —David Verba
> Adaptive Path

We created a set of paper prototypes and performed A/B testing with eight participants. We gave each participant a series of tasks that included adding a field using the more traditional model of static fields on the page and then asked them to use the new model, which allowed them to add fields on demand.

Half of the participants were shown the traditional model first and then the second. The other half was shown the reverse. We wanted to reduce bias and make sure we tested for multiple activities such as adding a new contact, adding additional phone numbers and email addresses to a contact, and adding speed dial numbers.

To our pleasant surprise, 12 out of our 12 participants immediately understood the preferred on-demand interaction model. Every single participant entered information into the text field, selected the Add action, and watched as we simulated the new field appearing.

I think a number of factors contributed to the success of this solution. First, there was only one option other than Save on the screen—the plus button, which is universally understood to mean Add. (But we also used a tooltip, just in case.) Essentially, the reduction of options lessened the opportunity for confusion. Second, the placement and proximity of the action to the input field helped communicate that "This action is related to this field."

We could have spent hours going round and round with the engineering team trying to sell our solution to them. The fact was that they needed to see an example and some results, not just hear about them. Once we showed them an example, they were more receptive, but still not convinced.

However, armed with 100 percent success from usability testing, there was very little room to argue that it wouldn't work, and they finally bought into the idea.

Prototyping allowed us to communicate our concept and make data-driven design decisions.

Type 5: Gauging Technical Feasibility and Value

Okay, so you have this really cool concept. You've worked with a visual designer, or perhaps you are the visual designer, to make it look really slick. But the ultimate question still remains: Can it be built?

I've seen countless cool designs buried by engineering and technology teams who were convinced that it just couldn't be built. If you're a designer and all you have is some really nice designs without a prototype, you're fighting a tough, uphill battle.

In some cases, you've got senior management on your side, and they can force engineering to build your design. But what if you don't? What if your design is really complex? What if it's not easily understood? These are all healthy indicators that should raise the "We need a prototype" red flag.

You don't have to have a production-quality prototype to gauge technical feasibility. In many, if not most cases, you can fake or simulate a great deal of the interaction. Simulations are enough to communicate your concept to management and engineering, get them to buy in, and help them determine if it's technically feasible or valuable enough to the business to invest in the concept.

Both of these notions of feasibility and value are equally important. The fact is that with software you can do anything you want—anything. All you have to do is invest enough time and effort. But that's the catch. To the business, it might not be worth the time and effort spent to develop a particular feature or a set of features. This is an argument of ROI for both engineering and the business.

For the engineers or technology team, their ROI interest is focused on the ratio of code to functionality. Their definition of what "works" tends to focus on a more technical definition. I once had an engineer who told me that for him, if he pulled up a terminal window and saw Apache was running on his box, that meant it was "working." For me, however, I expect to see Web pages rendering in my browser before I can say that it's actually "working." Both are technically definitions of Apache "working"—just two different perspectives.

For the business, their ROI interest is focused on the ratio of dollars out to dollars in. These dollars can be hard costs like buying hardware and software to get a system in place, or soft costs like ongoing maintenance or the cost of acquiring and maintaining customers. As much as we'd like to take a purist attitude that we should just make experiences better for the Zen of it, the fact is that at the end of the day a business has a financial responsibility to its employees that trumps the Zen factor.

Most of the prototypes we've built are production-level quality. In fact, HTML, CSS, and JavaScript are often used by the engineering team for final production. While this isn't typical, it's totally feasible.

When you build production-level prototypes, there's really no question of feasibility—the engineers are being handed a presentation layer with the "what's feasible" functionality already worked out. Our only hurdle here is to convince management that our concepts are solid and that the time needed by engineering to implement these concepts is of high value to the business. And that's a pretty easy hurdle to get over.

After we put the prototype into the hands of the users, they see an immediate benefit. Let them play with it for a couple of days, and they're entirely sold. Once the customer is sold on the prototype, management will follow soon.

Case Study: IntraLinks

by Todd Zaki Warfel

IntraLinks wanted to redesign their current Web application for virtual secure data rooms. The application hadn't changed much in the past five years, and it desperately needed an update. While they had their list of obvious things that needed fixing, they needed some outside assistance to uncover the not-so-obvious problems, so they contacted my company, Messagefirst. After four days of testing, we compiled a comprehensive list of what was working, what wasn't working, and a number of recommendations. Armed with the information, the design team at IntraLinks went to work. A year-and-a-half later, they had redesigned the application and produced a functional, high-fidelity RIA prototype.

I have to say, this was one of the most well-designed prototypes we've ever had the opportunity to work on. The design team at IntraLinks had made a radical shift from a Web-based application that behaved like a portal to a Web-based application that behaved like, well, an application.

The thing is, this prototype was an evolution of prototypes. It wasn't that IntraLinks had spent a year-and-a-half working on one prototype. They showed me a number of earlier iterations and designs. Many of those prototypes were very different from the final version they were ready to put in front of customers. They had put each of these previous prototypes through internal tests and had varying degrees of success and failure.

In some cases, the other designers on the team didn't feel the prototype was intuitive. In other cases, the senior executives didn't like the direction the prototype was taking the product. They had used a number of prototypes to incrementally and iteratively work their way through a design until they reached one they felt would be ready to put in front of customers for feedback. It was an evolutionary process.

Case Study: IntraLinks (continued)

You might be wondering "If it sounds so great, why did they test it?" Well, because it was a radically new design concept for them. In fact, it was several radically new design concepts. They wanted to see how their customers would react. Some of their current customers had been using the same version for over five years. Even though this new design was "better," if their customers couldn't use it, launching this new design could be disastrous.

First, the old design was very page-based—click a button, the page refreshes, do something and click another button, page refreshes again, click another button, page refreshes again. It wasn't necessarily broken, just outdated and inefficient. The new design, however, used a semi-stateless, screen-based rich interaction model often referred to as an *RIA*. This design was full of modern-day features like drag-and-drop, right-click, contextual menus, and auto-update. As with any extreme makeover, they wanted to see if they had done any harm. If they hadn't done harm, but had in fact improved it, how much had they improved it?

Second, they had a number of burning questions. Could customers get these new concepts? Would customers discover drag-and-drop? What about right-click and contextual menus? If they used these features in one area of the application, what other areas did they expect to use them? Which concepts didn't work, or simply needed some improvement?

Considering this radical shift and their questions, a functional high-fidelity prototype was the best way to test the design concepts before launching the product.

Overall, participants responded very positively to the new design. Several commented that it reminded them of their other applications. Many of the interactions, while different from their current IntraLinks, were familiar due to the similarity with Windows Explorer, Outlook, and other applications. The IntraLinks Design team was leveraging this existing knowledge built from interactions with other applications for their new design.

Case Study: IntraLinks (continued)

About half of the participants discovered the rich features like drag-and-drop, right-click, and contextual menus. Those who discovered these advanced features seemed to expect them from such a polished application. Those who didn't find them simply didn't expect to be able to do that type of interaction using a Web-based application. However, once they were shown, they were delighted and began looking for it throughout the application.

The prototype and testing were a huge success, validating many of their design decisions, proving they could successfully make the jump from portal-like to application, and providing valuable insights into additional new design concepts for system messaging and multistate transactions.

For IntraLinks, the ability to use prototyping as a way to work through the design process was paramount. They were able to use prototypes to explore a number of different solutions, which is especially valuable when attempting new design concepts or dealing with RIAs.

Summary

While prototypes can vary in fidelity and functionality, the most common uses for prototypes include:

- Creating a shared communication.

- Working through a design.

- Selling an idea to your boss or team members.

- Usability testing.

- Gauging technical feasibility and value.

You may find your prototypes fit more than one of these uses. In fact, that's pretty common. It's fairly easy to see how a prototype could serve as a shared communication platform, a vehicle for usability testing, and a way to test technical feasibility.

In the next chapter we'll look at eight guiding principles for better prototyping.

CHAPTER 4

Eight Guiding Principles

P rototyping isn't as hard as you think. In fact, it's pretty easy. Anyone can prototype. Just like anything else, the more you do it, the easier it gets. But here's the catch—it's just as easy to mess it up.

Most of the mistakes I've made, seen, or heard about didn't happen from selecting the wrong tool or method. Instead, most of the mistakes came from the following situations:

- Prototyping either too much or too little.

- Prototyping the wrong thing.

- Not setting expectations for what the prototype will be.

Effective prototyping is about finding balance and setting expectations. In this chapter, I'm going to reveal eight guiding principles I've developed for more effective prototyping. These principles apply, regardless of method or tool.

Best of all, whether you're a seasoned prototyper or just getting your feet wet, you'll benefit from the following eight guiding principles.

Principle 1: Understand Your Audience and Intent

This is the first and by far the most critical principle in the prototyping process. Understanding your audience *for* and the intent *of* the prototype drives every other aspect of the prototyping process. After you understand your audience and intent, you will be better equipped to:

- Determine what you need to prototype.

- Set appropriate expectations.

- Determine the right level of fidelity.

- Pick the right tool for the job.

Let's begin with addressing the question of audience, since it all starts here. When you understand who the audience is, you can determine what you need to prototype, how much you need to prototype, and what fidelity is appropriate for them.

If the audience is myself, another designer, or even an engineer, then a lo-fi paper prototype or a quick-and-dirty PowerPoint or HTML simulation is probably good enough. Those are mediums you can work with, you can understand, and that will get your point across without too much work.

However, if the audience for your prototype is a customer or a senior executive, chances are you'll need something more polished. A cocktail napkin sketch probably won't cut it.

When considering your audience, you should consider what medium or level of fidelity they will be comfortable with. If they can work with a few rough sketches on paper and you're confident that is all you need to communicate your concept to them, then go for it. If, on the other hand, your audience is going to struggle with that medium and you're going to struggle using it to communicate your concept to them, then pick a different medium or fidelity.

Once you understand your audience and the intent of your objective, you're ready to begin your planning phase and start prototyping.

Principle 2: Plan a Little— Prototype the Rest

Software systems change constantly and quickly. By planning a little and prototyping the rest, you work incrementally and iteratively, making up for the ever-changing environment.

The more work you do in the planning process, the better off you'll be. Of course, there is a point of diminishing return, so use some common sense.

I'm often asked how much planning should be done before you start prototyping. While there's no magic number, I plan up to approximately 70 percent of the design through sketching and then it's down to the business of prototyping.

Why 70 percent? There are two main reasons. First, since my goal is to get audience feedback, the faster I get it into their hands, the faster I can get feedback. Second, prototyping is a great tool for working through a design.

If I can get 70 percent of my design concept down on paper, then I can use prototyping to work through the rest.

In some ways, this makes prototyping a leap of faith. For those who are used to a waterfall method, or an environment where everything is "planned to a T" before you begin, this will probably make you a little uncomfortable. But just try it. Try planning about 70 percent of your prototype on a whiteboard or with paper and pencil and then starting prototyping. I'm confident you'll like the results.

Naturally, each prototype is created on a case-by-case basis. Sometimes, you might need to plan a little more, or you can plan a little less. Mission-critical systems, like a missile defense system or a system for monitoring a patient's vital signs in a hospital, will probably take a little more planning than say a video player.

There are other factors you might need to consider, such as environment, the tools you're using, and so on. Your magic number might not be 70 percent. Experiment a little with the amount of planning-to-prototyping you do. You'll find your sweet spot after a few tries.

When you plan a little and prototype the rest, you'll see the system come together quickly. You'll find your mistakes fast—and yes, there will be mistakes. You'll be able to fix those mistakes with less total time and effort. Best of all, you'll have something your audience can play with and ultimately give you feedback on that you can use in a timely manner.

Principle 3: Set Expectations

Setting expectations is based on a psychological technique known as *priming*. When you prime your audience, you guide their attention and focus.

Let's try a little experiment. I've prototyped a shopping cart and checkout experience for the ecommerce area of a mobile service provider. In just a minute, I'm going to show you a prototype of some of the concepts, which will highlight a few key features, such as featured products during the shopping experience and promoting phone accessories during the checkout process. Both of these key features will help increase profitability through add-on sales.

See how this works? I haven't even shown you a prototype yet, but you have an expectation of what you're going to see. You can even start to imagine them.

When I show you the prototype, you're more likely to focus on looking for the featured product and promoted accessories than you are on what's in the header and footer or what color the checkout button is.

Setting expectations typically boils down to two things: fidelity and functionality. For companies who are just starting to prototype, this is one of the most common mistakes and the easiest to avoid.

Remember the first guiding principle—know your audience and intent. If this is the first experience your audience has with prototyping, it's critical you set their expectations of what to expect from the prototype. Reactions to a prototype are more favorable if the audience can predict with some degree of certainty what they will and won't see.

By setting the expectation up-front, you avoid the rabbit-hole discussions about detailed interactions or pieces of functionality that simply haven't been prototyped yet. Not to say that they won't come up, because they will. By setting expectations correctly in the beginning, you give yourself an easy out—it's not part of the prototype yet, but you can work it into the next release.

After you've primed your audience and set their expectations, launch the prototype and show them the demo. Don't be afraid to discuss things that aren't in the prototype at this stage, but try to keep the discussion focused on what is in this particular prototype. Remind them that this is a prototype and that some things might not be fully fleshed out yet.

TIP CREATE A PLAYLIST SCRIPT

Write a short "playlist" of the most important features that you want to highlight when demo'ing your prototype. It will help keep you on track and ensure that you don't miss anything during the presentation.

Principle 4: You Can Sketch

We're so lo-fi it's not even funny.

—Scott Matthews
Xplane

At a small conference named Overlap, David Gray of Xplane asked by a show of hands who could draw. Of the 40 plus people attending only a few raised their hands. Then Dave asked another question, "Who here could draw when they were a kid?" Everyone in the room raised their hands. His response was simple, "So, what happened between then and now that you lost your ability to draw?" Nobody really had a good response.

Dave, with some help from his colleague Scott Matthews, went on to show how you could draw anything you need with a few simple shapes—a square, a triangle, a circle, and a straight line. He showed how you could draw a person running similar to the sketch in Figure 4.1.

FIGURE 4.1
Sketch of a running man.

You probably won't find that particular drawing in the next issue of any anatomy book, but we all get the picture. And that's what prototypes are—showing, communicating, and helping your audience get the picture.

I don't consider myself to be an artist, but I do sketch—a lot. Some of my sketches are more refined than others. Sometimes I'll put actual words for field labels, and other times I'll just draw lines to represent that a label needs to be there, as shown in Figure 4.2.

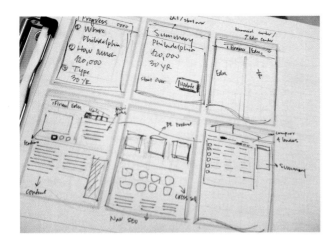

FIGURE 4.2
Sketch with lines for labels and text.

If I'm doing an ultra quick-and-dirty sketch, where I'm really only interested in carving out parts of the screen real estate for functionality, I'll go lower fidelity and typically just use lines. Or if I'm live sketching with another designer or the client, I'll use the same technique.

If the actual order of the fields is critical and I need to communicate that, I'll go a little higher fidelity and either write the labels in or possibly open Illustrator and use it to sketch out the screen.

This decision often comes back to the first principle: Know your audience and intent. If it's just me, I'm often fine with lines and boxes, no labels needed. (I'll have a list of those written on a separate piece of paper.) If it's someone else who's consuming it, I'll usually put in a little more effort and write out the labels.

Remember if you could draw when you were a kid, you can draw now. Your goal isn't to create an illustration for the *New Yorker*, it's to communicate your idea. After all, it's just a prototype. Which brings us to Principle 5.

> **TIP** WHITEBOARDING AJAX
>
> Try using a whiteboard for sketching. You can simulate interactions and AJAX transitions through erasing and redrawing.

Principle 5: It's a Prototype— Not the Mona Lisa

Prototypes by their very nature are somewhat incomplete, sketchy versions of the final product. They're not perfect. They don't have to be. They're not meant to be. In fact, a slightly rough and sketchy prototype is often better for getting feedback.

If it's unfinished, participants are more apt to give their feedback. They don't feel that all the decisions have been made and are subsequently set in stone.

Admittedly, there are cases when you need something more refined. A sketchy prototype at a trade show probably isn't going to cut it. And your CEO might have some trouble envisioning the final product from a sketch or a black-and-white version of the prototype. So, again, use some common sense judgment.

What I can tell you with great confidence, however, is this—in most cases, your prototype doesn't have to be a Mona Lisa—good enough is good enough.

You're not shooting for perfection here—*it's a prototype.* You're shooting for something that takes the least amount of time and effort required to communicate to your audience the core concept of your idea. All you need is the right level of fidelity. No more. No less.

Principle 6: If You Can't Make It, Fake It

This is probably the biggest hurdle for newbies venturing into prototyping. Whenever I give a talk or workshop on prototyping, I start by asking the audience a few questions:

- How many people feel comfortable writing code (either HTML or something else)?

- How many people have prototyped in some way, shape, or form in the past (either PowerPoint, HTML, Dreamweaver, PDFs, etc.)?

In general, I find that the more designers there are in the room, the fewer people I find that feel comfortable writing code of some kind and the fewer people who have prototyped or feel comfortable prototyping. This typically comes down to the myth that if you can't write code, you can't prototype. And this has increased with RIAs. If you can't write JavaScript, then you can't prototype.

> As prototyping gets quicker and easier, it really does save a lot of time to quickly prototype the ideas people have and show them in use. It fleshes out the wheat from the chaff very effectively.
>
> —Baruch Sachs
> Director, Human Factors Design and Pegasystems

If you can't code, or can't make it, there are a number of options for faking it.

- You can fake it with a series of JPEG screens. Use Dreamweaver to create image maps and link them together. You don't write a single line of code, but you can get feedback on the interaction and flow to see if it makes sense.

- Use Fireworks' built-in capabilities to link between pages and frames; then generate a clickable HTML prototype.

- Use your favorite PDF creation tool or Adobe Acrobat and link them together for the same result.

- Use PowerPoint to link a series of still screens together.

- Use a series of HTML screens to simulate AJAX and other rich interactions.

At a talk I did for DC Refresh, I discussed a recent prototype we had done for a client. I talked about some of the rich interactions we had incorporated into the prototype with the help of the popular Prototype JavaScript library.

I told the audience I would show them a few basic show/hide interactions we had built into the prototype. I also told them that some of the interactions they would see were real and some were faked. And then I showed them the show/hide functionality for advanced search in Figures 4.3 and 4.4.

FIGURE 4.3
Basic search (hide).

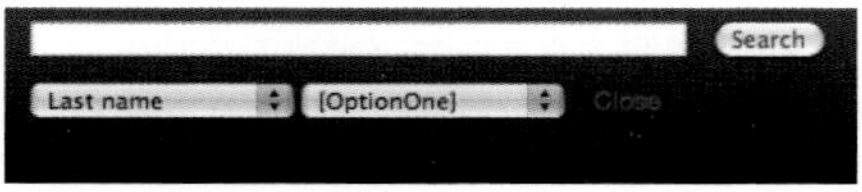

FIGURE 4.4
Advanced search (show).

I toggled back and forth several times between the two states—showing advanced search and then hiding it. Then I pointed out the two different URLs. This AJAX simulation wasn't AJAX at all, but rather two different screens linked together. It was faked.

The thing is, it didn't matter that it was faked. The audience got the concept of show/hide for advanced search.

There are a number of tools out there to fake it, and more than likely you have more than one of them at your disposal. As long as you prime your audience first, set their expectations for what they're going to see, and then have a simulation that shows what you've described, you're good to go.

Principle 7: Prototype Only What You Need

More often than not, the prototypes you build are going to be pieces of the entire system. You don't need to build the entire system and get it to work to explore a design or to get feedback on it. In fact, trying to build the entire system loses the inherent benefits of rapid iteration.

If your ultimate goal is to use the prototypes for testing, chances are you're going to test five to six scenarios. In that case, you only need to build what's needed for those five to six scenarios.

What happens if a test participant clicks on part of the prototype that hasn't been built? It's a prototype. Prototypes are inherently incomplete. If a participant clicks on a feature that isn't built, you use that as an opportunity to explore how he might expect it to behave.

By prototyping only the pieces you need, your investment is greatly reduced in a number of ways—cost, time, and effort. Additionally, since it takes less time to build only what you need, you'll get feedback faster and move on. If the small piece you build works, then you can keep going. If not, then there's no major loss, and you can try something else.

Principle 8: Reduce Risk— Prototype Early and Often

We have these huge firms cranking out wireframes, building things, and discovering problems way too late.

—Anders Ramsay

As we've already discussed, prototyping has a number of advantages, one of which is the low investment-to-benefit ratio. Let's look at two development models—one is the traditional waterfall method and the other utilizes rapid iterative prototyping.

In a traditional waterfall method, all of the system's features and functions are planned before any development begins. This often leads to a six- to nine-month planning cycle before any actual work on the system begins.

In environments that move slowly or don't change much, this might not be an issue. In today's software industry, however, nine months is a lifetime—an entire company can be created bought, sold, and go under in nine months.

But let's pretend your entire industry moves at the same slow snail's pace that you do. In that case, you're so heavily invested at this point that it's nearly impossible or just not feasible to change direction. The ship has already sailed, and there's no changing course—there's no turning back.

This is a very costly model. More often than not, mistakes are made, and the recovery is too costly, as high as 100 percent. As such, these mistakes are left in the system for the end user to try to work around.

The other approach takes a more agile approach. You chip away at bite-sized pieces and use an incremental, iterative, and evolutionary approach. By using this approach with prototyping, you've only invested in small amounts. Reducing your investment reduces your risk.

You're committing a few weeks at a time to a small set of concepts to see if they're going to work or not. If they don't work, there's much less damage that's done, because you're only a few weeks away from pulling them and replacing them with something that works better. You're not stuck for another six, nine, twelve, or eighteen months.

If they do work, you see an immediate benefit. You can make rapid iterative adjustments. You can stay ahead of your market, often leading the space. You can be more proactive and less reactive.

This is an area where prototyping really shines. You make small investments with a significant return. That return can be positive or negative. If it's positive, then all the better. If it's negative, then your risk is substantially reduced because you'll find it early enough in the process and be able to replace it quickly.

The earlier in the development process you catch a mistake, the easier and less costly it is to correct your mistake. And don't kid yourself—you will make mistakes. By some estimates, changes during design can be as low as 10 percent, and during development or after product launch, your costs skyrocket to 100 percent.

When you start prototyping early and often, you'll reduce your risk and save yourself a great deal of headache, time, effort, and money.

Summary

Making mistakes in the prototype process is common. Avoiding them is pretty easy when you remember these eight guiding principles:

- Understand your audience and intent.

- Plan a little and prototype the rest.

- Set expectations.

- You can sketch.

- It's a prototype, not the Mona Lisa.

- If you can't make, fake it.

- Prototype only what you need.

- Reduce risk. Prototype early and often.

There you have it. Those are the eight guiding principles for effective prototyping. In the next chapter, I'll discuss the most common prototyping tools being used in the UX community, so you can decide which tool is right for you.

CHAPTER 5

Picking the
Right Tool

In 2008, I ran the first survey on prototyping for this book. My goal was to understand what tools UX people are using for prototyping, why they're using those tools, and what they want from those tools. I also wanted to see how my experiences and choices compared to the rest of the UX community.

Roughly 200 people responded from a variety of UX backgrounds, including researchers, designers, developers, product managers, and business analysts.

This chapter discusses the results of that survey and offers some guidance for selecting the right prototyping tool for your environment.

Influencers

When I started this book, most of my prototyping was done using HTML and CSS. Honestly, I had to fake the majority of my AJAX interactions and transitions. My JavaScript skills were pretty mediocre.

One day, I decided to bite the bullet and get familiar with the Prototype and script.aculo.us JavaScript library. It took a few days of trial and error before I finally got a handle on things. I haven't looked back since.

At the time of writing this chapter, most of my prototyping is still done using HTML, CSS, and Prototype and script.aculo.us. My JavaScript skills have evolved, and I no longer have to fake AJAX.

The available prototyping options continue to grow. By the time I finish this book, my tools of choice could very well change or evolve again. I've been playing with the jQuery JavaScript library. Adobe just released a new version of Fireworks and Flash. Who knows what will be available?

So why choose HTML, Flash, Fireworks, Axure, or something else? According to the survey, these are the top influencers that drive tool choice, in order of importance:

1.   Familiarity and availability

2.   Time and effort to produce a working prototype

3.   Creating usable prototype for testing

4. Price

5. Learning curve

6. Ability to create own GUI widgets

7. Available on my platform

8. Collaborative/remote design capabilities

9. Built-in solutions/patterns for AJAX transitions

10. Built-in GUI widgets

11. Creating usable source code

I can definitely find my own influencers in that list with one exception—knowing the audience and intent. This is my number one concern. But my other concerns, like familiarity, availability, comfort, availability of GUI widgets and AJAX, or ability to create my own are definitely in that list. They just might be in a slightly different order.

You'll see this list again later in the book. I'm going to use it to evaluate a number of different prototyping tools.

You may notice the presence of creating usable source code. You may also notice that it's at the bottom of the list. This one's a bit tricky.

Creating prototypes that are reusable for production isn't something that's commonly done or recommended. There are several reasons for this. Prototyping is a rapid, iterative process. It's a process for exploring ideas, failing often, and learning quickly. If you're focused on creating production-level code, you start to lose some of the value of rapid iteration.

On the other hand, if you can produce reusable source code with very little or no additional effort, then your prototyping tool has the added value of development time.

At the time of this book's publication, there isn't a dedicated prototyping tool for non-coders that can create rapid prototypes with little effort and produce reusable source code. If you want a prototyping tool that produces reusable source code, you'll have to learn to code HTML or use a development framework like Ruby on Rails.

What Tools Are People Using?

As I expected, the usual suspects like paper, PowerPoint, Flash, and HTML showed up on the most common tools list. Also, not surprising is that participants used more than one tool. For instance, they might use a combination of paper for sketching and then go into Photoshop and finally HTML.

In the past couple of years, a couple of newcomers have hit the scene and continue to gain traction, namely Axure RP and Fireworks. While Fireworks has been around for some time, only recently has it gained built-in prototyping capabilities. Here's a breakdown of the most common tools being used for prototyping in the UX field as of 2008 (see Table 5.1).[1]

TABLE 5.1 SURVEY RESULTS OF COMMON PROTOTYPING TOOL USAGE

Paper	77.0%
Visio	59.0%
PowerPoint	43.0%
Dreamweaver	47.0%
Axure	30.0%
OmniGraffle	30.0%
Illustrator	23.0%
Flash	21.0%
Acrobat	19.0%
Fireworks	18.0%
InDesign	12.0%
Photoshop	10.0%
Other HTML editor	4.0%
Keynote	3.0%
Flex	2.0%
Blend	0.2%
iRise	0.1%
Other (Excel, FileMaker)	0.1%

---

1   Participants were allowed, but not required to select their most common tools up to a maximum of three—one participant could select Paper, Visio, and HTML. Since participants could select up to three tools, the percentages will exceed 100. toddwarfel.com/archives/first-prototyping-survey-results/

I'm sure you can see a number of familiar tools in that list. Did you notice any surprises?

Probably the biggest surprise to me was the number of people who use Visio for prototyping. I expected to see Visio, but didn't expect nearly 60 percent. Another surprise was the presence of Excel and FileMaker for prototyping. While this made up less than one percent of respondents, I was surprised to see it at all. Finally, the sheer number of prototyping tools being used for prototyping was a bit surprising—over 26 total if you include the items listed under Other.

What Kinds of Prototypes Are They Making?

Paper continues to be at the top of the list. The continued growth of AJAX libraries like Prototype and jQuery, combined with the increasing number of auto-generating tools like Axure, iRise, and Fireworks, has made creating interactive prototypes easier than ever.

Ruby on Rails (RoR) is another one that has seen an increase in use for prototyping. Rails is a rapid application development framework, which makes it an ideal tool for both prototyping and production. Rails maintains all the advantages of HTML with the added capability to use dynamic data.

Here's a breakdown in Table 5.2 of the most common types of prototypes that people in the UX community are building.

TABLE 5.2 SURVEY RESULTS OF COMMON
TYPES OF PROTOTYPES

Paper	81.0%
Hand-coded HTML	58.0%
Auto-generated (Axure, iRise, Visio, Fireworks, or similar)	39.0%
Clickable screenshots using HTML	34.0%
Flash, Flex, AIR, or Blend	27.0%
Keynote or PowerPoint	24.0%
Clickable PDFs	21.0%
Production environments (Rails, Java, .Net, PHP, Xcode)	9.0%
3D models (cardboard, foam core)	2.0%

Most of my prototypes are created using HTML and AJAX. I use an HTML/CSS framework we developed in-house at Messagefirst combined with either the Prototype or jQuery JavaScript library. While my prototypes are all hand-coded, leveraging an existing, well-tested framework and JavaScript library means I can maintain a rapid, iterative approach.

In some cases, I need to use something other than HTML, for example, for mobile or TV. If I need to prototype for mobile, I typically use paper or Flash. If I need to prototype, say, for instance, a DVR interface, I use Flash or Keynote.

Summary

I've never been one to do something just because others are doing it. And in the case of prototyping that hasn't changed.

Most of the prototypes I create are production level HTML prototypes, but I wouldn't recommend that for most people. I choose that method because it's the method that suits my needs and I'm comfortable with the tools. So, how would I recommend you select a prototyping method or tool? Well, consider the following:

1. **Audience:** Who is going to view or interact with the prototype?

2. **Intent:** Think back to the five types of prototypes. Which of these do you need?

3. **Familiarity and learnability:** Are you familiar with the method or tool, or willing to learn it?

4. **Cost:** Don't just think about the license cost, also consider the cost of downtime if you need to learn it.

5. **Collaboration:** Do you need it? If so, your choices are significantly limited.

6. **Distribution:** How will you share it with others?

7. **Throwaway versus resusable:** If you need reusable source code, then your choices are limited. If you're going to throw it away, which is more likely, then your options are wide open.

You'll find a comparison matrix inside the front cover of this book, which will help you evaluate the methods and tools reviewed in this book.

At this point in the book, you've completed all the overview material for prototyping. From this point forward, I'm going to focus on specific tools, evaluating them based on the criteria listed in this chapter, and I will also cover a few tips and techniques for each of the tools.

Paper

Prototyping Models

Paper	●
Digital	◐
Narrative	●
Interactive	◐
Rapid	●

Stages

Early	●
Late	◐

Compatibility & Cost

Mac	N/A
Windows	N/A
Cost	Free

Portability & Use

Web	●
Mobile	●
Gestural	○
Reusable Code	○

Collaboration, Distribution, & Traceability

Collaboration	●
Distribution	○
Traceability	○

HOW TO READ THIS TABLE

● Ideal   ◐ Capable, but Not Ideal   ○ Not Suitable

CHAPTER 6

Paper and Other Analog Methods

FIGURE 6.1
Sample paper
prototype of the
iPhone application,
Things.

aper prototyping is the most versatile method around. Paper is ideal for creating everything from Web interfaces to gestural interactions.

Paper prototyping has been around for decades, gaining popularity primarily in academic institutions and large corporations like IBM, Digital, and Sun in the 1990s. Back then you were likely to get some strange looks if you said you did paper prototyping. My oh my, how times have changed!

Paper is the most common method in use today. In fact, 76 percent of the survey respondents stated they use paper prototyping. Of all the methods I've used over the years, paper continues to be one of my favorites. Sure, paper and other analog tools have shortcomings just like any other method. The advantages are so great, however, that it's silly not to have it in your prototyping toolkit.

In this chapter, we're going to explore the strengths and challenges of using paper, when to consider paper, what to put in your paper prototyping kit, and a number of techniques for paper prototyping, including AJAX-style simulations.

Strengths

Some of the more obvious strengths of paper prototyping include the following:

- **Versatile.** Paper is one of the few tools that is equally well suited for prototyping software and physical devices, especially mobile and gestural interactions.

- **Fast.** Just about any interaction you can dream up can be prototyped in just a few minutes.

- **Cheap.** There's no software license costs. You probably already have all the tools you'll need sitting around your home or office.

- **Easy.** There's a near zero barrier to entry. Anyone can do it.

- **Manipulate on the fly.** What if in the middle of testing your prototype, a participant comes up with a design concept you didn't think of? No problem. You can edit your paper prototype on the fly and the participant can even help.

- **Collaborative.** It's great for participatory design with other team members or usability test participants.

- **Not bound by hardware or software limitations.** With paper prototyping, unlike other prototyping tools, you're not bound to prebuilt GUI widgets or interactions. Paper gives you a true blank canvas to explore any interaction you can dream up.

- **Anywhere, anytime.** Paper prototyping doesn't require a computer, and can be done anywhere, anytime.

Weaknesses

While one of the most popular methods, and one of my personal favorites, paper prototyping isn't without its weaknesses, including the following:

- **Distributed work.** For obvious reasons, it's hard for geographically distributed teams to work with paper prototypes. Passing paper prototypes back and forth between the U.S. and Ireland, for example, will prove a bit challenging. Screen sharing software like Adobe Acrobat Connect or WebEx makes it easier.

- **Imagination required.** It's not a real iPhone, so you'll need to bring your imagination to the table.

- **Visual aesthetics.** If you want to evaluate the impact of color of visual aesthetics on the usability and experience, paper probably isn't the right choice.

Paper Prototyping on the Fly

I was working on a digital voice product for a large telecom client several years ago. We wanted to test some of the design concepts. Since we had an existing set of wireframes, paper prototyping seemed to be the most logical solution.

One of the design concepts was blocking a phone number. Imagine you're at dinner and you get a call from one of those 866 telemarketing numbers. You'd like to block that number from ever calling you again. We had designed a solution to allow you to sign-in to your digital voice service and add that number to a block list.

We ran the first participant through the scenario and asked him to show us how he might expect to block the number. He did something unexpected, as participants often do, and attempted to right-click on the phone number expecting to see a list of options, including "Block this number." This wasn't one of the solutions we had designed. It made total sense, but wasn't one of the concepts we had even considered. (This was before AJAX hit the scene.)

The person assisting me gave me a look of "What do we do now?" I simply picked up a yellow sticky note, drew a few options on it, and put it on top of the number and asked "Something like this?" The participant smiled and replied, "Yeah. Yeah, just like that."

The remaining nine participants did the same thing. Paper prototyping allowed us to create an alternate solution in a matter of seconds—something we never could have done with a digital prototype.

Essential Paper Prototyping Kit

Whenever I teach a paper prototyping workshop, I make a kit for every table or group. That kit includes the following:

- **Paper.** A stack of 8 1/2 × 11 plain white paper. We use these for the base of each design.

- **Transparencies.** A stack of 8 1/2 × 11 transparency sheets. These are handy for simulating navigation rollovers and the popular Lightbox effect.

- **Index cards.** Standard 3 × 5 plain cards will do. Index cards are used for a variety of things, like dialog windows and GUI widgets. We typically provide the kind that are lined on one side and blank on the other. The subtle blue lines help when you're writing dialog messages.

- **Post-it notes.** I tend to lean toward yellow, but any color will do. Post-its are handy for a number of things like displaying changing states in tiles on the page, highlighting selected items on a screen, or dialog windows.

- **Colored pens or markers.** I include fine point and broad point markers in the kits. Each kit contains black, blue, red, and green. Most of the sketching is done with the black or blue, error messages in red, and success messages in green.

- **Scotch tape or a glue stick.** Great for providing a little bit of stick to GUI widgets. When using paper for RIA prototypes, a little bit of glue stick on the back of a tile is a great way to allow participants to move things around or show changes in state, while keeping the other pieces in place.

- **Flat dental tape.** This is the one magical trick I put into the kits. Flat dental tape is great for simulating animations. In the past, I've used it as a way to drag the scrubber of an audio player or pull a strip of photos through a photo gallery.

TIP USE ILLUSTRATOR OR VISIO TO CREATE YOUR GUI WIDGETS

Use your favorite drawing program to draw the basic structure of your page and GUI widgets. Print out several copies and sketch your prototype ideas on the printouts. This gives your paper prototypes some basic structure, while still providing the flexibility to cut them up or throw them away.

Progressive Paper Prototyping

Okay, this is the fun part of this chapter. This is where you get to see a number of hands-on tricks for creating richer paper prototypes. We're going to start with something basic, like a form design, and move onto more advanced techniques like simulating AJAX. Let's start by looking at a number of tips for creating GUI widgets for your paper prototypes. You can download an Illustrator file with sample GUI widgets at **☎ rosenfeldmedia. com/books/downloads/prototyping/Paper_Prototype_GUI.ai.**

Paper Prototyping Basics

Think of your paper prototype as a recipe—you start with a few basic raw ingredients and then combine them to create something really amazing.

Your basic ingredients for any paper prototype are the *shell* of the prototype and the *GUI widgets*. These can be hand drawn, as shown in Figure 6.2, or printed like Figure 6.3. Just make sure you have both on and off states for each element.

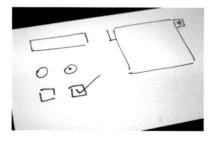

FIGURE 6.2
Hand-drawn
application GUI
widgets.

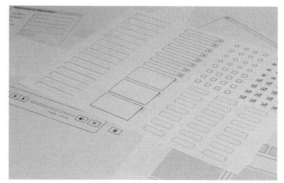

FIGURE 6.3
Printed application GUI
widgets.

TIP HANDLEBARS

Bend the side of your GUI widgets up to form a right-angled handle, as shown in Figure 6.4. This makes it easier to pick them up during testing.

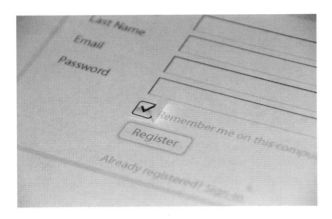

FIGURE 6.4
Close-up of handlebar for GUI widgets.

Now that you have most of the elements you need, let's start with something basic like a registration form and move on from there.

Paper Prototyping a Basic Registration Form

A registration form is pretty common for Web-based applications and ecommerce sites, which makes it a great starting point. Let's create a registration form that has the following capabilities for your customers:

- Enter first and last name
- Enter email address (used for sign-in and to recover password)
- Enter a password
- Be remembered in the future
- Register
- Sign-in if the visitor is already registered

Figure 6.5 shows the example I've created. Looks pretty straightforward, right?

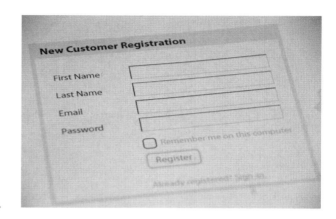

FIGURE 6.5
Paper prototype of a
basic registration form.

Communicating Changes in State

Reflecting a change in state is one of the key differences between sketches and prototypes. These changes in state can be macro, like an entire screen change, or micro, like selecting a checkbox.

When working with paper prototypes, changes in state can be reflected easily by writing on the prototype. If test participants want to select a checkbox, they just mark it with a pen. This works for selecting the checkbox, but what if they want to deselect it?

Remember those GUI widgets we created earlier? If one of your test participants wants to select the checkbox, just drop a paper selected checkbox on top, like in Figure 6.6. This reflects the change in state and is easy to undo.

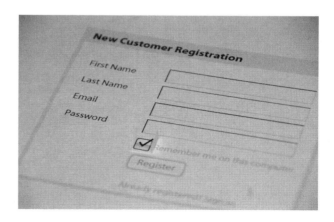

FIGURE 6.6
Paper prototype with
selected checkbox GUI
widget in place.

This effect is equally useful for other GUI elements like select menus, radio buttons, and audio controls.

While you could use this effect to show a hover or highlight effect, I prefer something different—a transparency.

Transparencies are one of my favorite little tricks. They're incredibly flexible. I use them for a number of effects, including hover states for navigation (see Figure 6.7), highlighting input fields that have focus, and overlay effects.

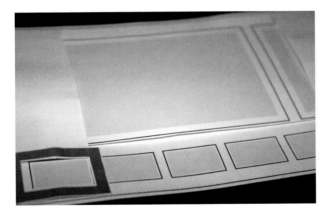

FIGURE 6.7
Here I use a transparency to show a selected thumbnail in a photo gallery.

Applying this technique to our registration form, you'll see how we can simulate something like in-line contextual help. Let's say you want to show that when a participant selects an input field, that field is highlighted and a little contextual help overlay displays at the right.

To accomplish this effect, we'll need the following:

- Yellow highlighter and piece of transparency or a piece of colored transparency

- Piece of 3 × 5 card for the overlay

- Tape or rubber cement

First, cut out a small piece of transparency about the size of your input field. Next, cut out an overlay section for your in-line contextual help. Tape the contextual help bubble to your transparency, and you'll have something similar to Figure 6.8. Don't forget to fold one side of the transparency to give yourself a handle.

As the participant moves through the form, you can slide the transparency down, simulating in-line contextual help. For fields that don't have help, simply use your handle and pick up the transparency. There you have it—in-line contextual help.

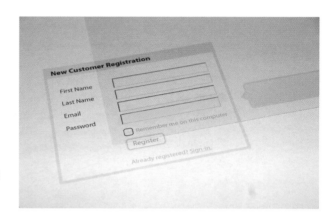

FIGURE 6.8
Highlight selected field and display in-line contextual help.

Advanced Paper Prototyping Techniques

One of the most common myths of paper prototyping is that you can't use it to simulate interactivity like an AJAX-style show/hide or scrolling a photo gallery. These are easier than you might think, and they build on some of the basic prototyping techniques I've already covered.

One of the most common AJAX-style[1] techniques is show/hide where a user clicks a link to display additional content and then clicks again to hide it. This is probably one of the easiest effects to simulate. All you have to do is fold a piece of paper.

---

1   I use the term AJAX-style here, because purists will argue true AJAX transfers information to and from the server. In many cases an AJAX effect is achieved without actually communicating with the server.

In this example, I'm going to use a voicemail widget I've created for a Web-based application. The default state of the widget displays each voicemail with some summary information. If you select the expand button, the area below the selected voicemail expands to show additional information and actions, as shown in Figure 6.9. Selecting the button again collapses it, hiding the additional information.

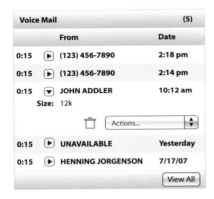

FIGURE 6.9
Expanded state of the widget.

To accomplish a show/hide effect, I'll start with a printed copy of the widget and make two creases: one above and one below the content I want to show and hide (see Figure 6.10).

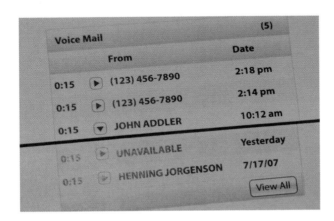

FIGURE 6.10
Folds created to simulate show/hide effect.

Beyond Boundaries

At the Interactions '09 conference in Savannah, I taught a paper prototyping workshop and asked the participants to create a photo gallery carousel. I showed them the Yahoo! User Interface (YUI!) carousel widget as an example. Most of the groups created a pretty standard sliding image gallery, similar to the YUI! carousel (see Figure 6.11).

FIGURE 6.11
Basic carousel paper prototype.

There were two groups, however, who created something totally and completely unexpected—shockingly brilliant (see Figure 6.12).

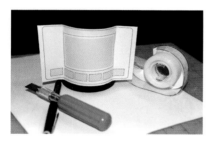

FIGURE 6.12
3D carousel paper prototype

The participants in my workshops never cease to surprise and amaze me. Whether it was due to a misunderstanding, or their vivid imagination, I don't know, but they had created a 3D carousel—something you would never ever try with HTML.

When working within a particular software program or programming language, we often constrain our ideas to what that environment natively supports. If it supports 2D, we think in terms of 2D. If it doesn't support it, or if it's difficult, we are more likely to stick to the native, pre-built, canned solutions and less likely to push, bend, break, and innovate.

To simulate the effect, I start with the paper folded over, which is the default hidden state of the tile. To simulate the show effect, I unfold the paper, to expand the widget and display the additional content. It's really that easy.

Another common simulation is the slide effect. This is useful for simulating a photo gallery, the movement of an audio/video player, the iTunes cover flow effect, or the motion scroll found on the iPhone. This takes a little more work than show/hide, but it is still pretty easy to accomplish.

In this example, we're going to create a photo gallery. As the user selects a different image by sliding the selector, I can move the photos through the viewing window automatically.

To start, you'll need to create three elements: a viewing window, a thumbnail selector, and a strip of photos. I've created mine in Illustrator, as shown in Figure 6.13.

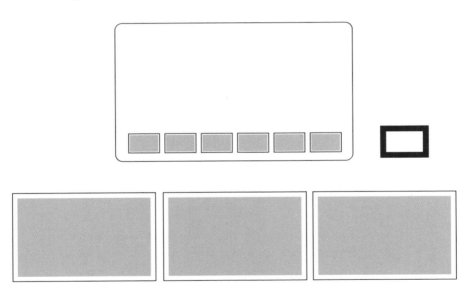

FIGURE 6.13
Components for a sliding photo gallery.

Next, cut a slit at each end of the viewing window. You'll need to make sure it's wide enough to fit your photo strip through it. Then slide the strip through the two slits so that it's viewable in the window with one side sticking out. You should have something that resembles Figure 6.14.

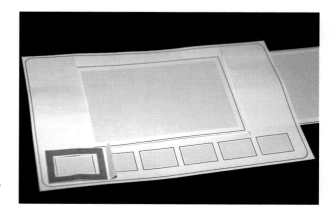

FIGURE 6.14
Photo strip slid into the viewing window.

As the participant moves the selector across the thumbnails at the bottom, you can slide the larger photo strip through the window to simulate the effect. For an additional bonus, use a piece of flat dental floss taped to the back of your photo strip to pull the strip back and forth.

TIP GIVE YOUR SLIDERS SOME BREAKS

When making sliders, fold each end over like you would to create a handle for a GUI widget. Instead of acting like a handle, this folded-over area will catch the edge of the viewing window, acting as a stop and preventing it from pulling all the way through.

I've used this technique in usability testing to evaluate automatic versus manual transitions on a screen. I created a similar widget that would rotate featured stories on a home page.

For half the participants, I presented the home page and let them select an item before moving the featured story. During the conversation, I asked if they had any feedback on making this automatic instead of manual, and their responses were rather tame.

For the other half, I presented the home page and after a few seconds automatically moved the featured story by pulling a string. Several of these participants got excited after seeing the effect. They became curious and asked if the real home page would do that.

By showing the actual effect, I was able to obtain richer feedback than I did by just describing it. And I was able to accomplish it with just a few minutes of effort and absolutely zero coding.

Paper Prototyping for Physical Devices

Paper prototyping isn't limited to software interfaces. In fact, it's one of the few methods that bridge the gap between software and hardware prototyping. If you're doing any work in physical devices like handheld, mobile, or even machines like ATMs, you should consider paper.

Since physical devices are more tangible than software interfaces, the value of paper prototyping is even greater. With paper, you can create a physical model of a hardware device like an iPhone, shown in Figure 6.15, or even an ATM or subway ticketing system, shown in Figure 6.16.

IMAGE BY STEVEN TOOMEY.

FIGURE 6.15
iPhone paper prototype. www.flickr.com/photos/typeweight/
357099407/in/set-72157594476948766/

PAPER AND OTHER ANALOG METHODS   79

FIGURE 6.16
Subway ticketing paper prototype.
www.flickr.com/photos/knute/2247602574/

Simulating screen changes on physical devices is fairly easy as well. Just follow the same basic principles I covered earlier for slide effects.

First, create a frame for the viewing window and tape it over the physical device. Next, cut a slit in the top of the viewing area and slide your screens in and out of the viewing area to simulate the screen changes. Once again, no programming is involved.

GUI Magnets

GUI magnets are small, flexible magnets with GUI-elements on them. You can use them for collaborative brainstorming on whiteboards and easily drag-and-drop different magnets to find the best interface prototype. GUI magnets are available online at shop.guimagnets.com/.

Also, you might want to check out this book for additional information: *Paper Prototyping: The Fast and Easy Way to Design and Refine User Interfaces* by Carolyn Snyder paperprototyping.com.

Summary

How's your paper prototyping confidence? Feel like you could tackle just about anything? Now you can see why I think paper is such a powerful method and tool.

- It's fast, cheap (basically free), and easy.

- You can use it anywhere and anytime—no computer necessary.

- It's one of the few tools that's suitable for collaborative design.

PowerPoint & Keynote

Prototyping Models

Paper	◐
Digital	◐
Narrative	●
Interactive	◐
Rapid	●

Stages

Early	●
Late	◐

Compatibility & Cost

Mac	●
Windows	●
Cost	$79-679

Portability & Use

Web	●
Mobile	◐
Gestural	○
Reusable Code	○

Collaboration, Distribution, & Traceability

Collaboration	◐
Distribution	◐
Traceability	◐

HOW TO READ THIS TABLE

● Ideal ◐ Capable, but Not Ideal ○ Not Suitable

CHAPTER 7

PowerPoint and Keynote

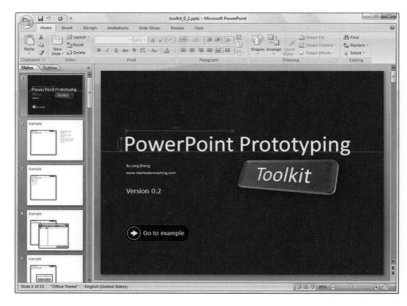

FIGURE 7.1
Example of a prototype dashboard created with PowerPoint 2007.
www.istartedsomething.com/20071018/powerpoint-prototype-toolkit-01/

Microsoft PowerPoint and Apple Keynote are more than just tools for making great presentations. While not as robust as Axure, Flash, or HTML, PowerPoint and Keynote have become popular prototyping tools.

How popular? Well, over 40 percent of the industry uses them for some form of prototyping. In fact, PowerPoint played a pivotal role in the design process of Windows 7, Windows Live, Internet Explorer, and Expression Blend at Microsoft.[1]

PowerPoint is just about as omnipresent as Microsoft Word. It comes with Microsoft Office, which is on just about every working professional's computer on the planet. For those of us who choose not to use Microsoft Office, but instead opt for Apple iWork, there's Keynote.

---

1   www.istartedsomething.com/20071014/microsoft-prototpying-powerpoint/
    Please note that the word "prototyping" must be misspelled as above in order to work.

Have you ever had a client or a designer give you a set of Photoshop files and ask you to create a prototype? You could use the old slap-and-map method—for example, stitch them together with Dreamweaver and create image maps. Or you could use PowerPoint or Keynote.

In this chapter, we're going to explore using PowerPoint and Keynote to create narrative and interactive prototypes. I'll also discuss techniques you can use to create AJAX simulations.

Strengths

Here are some of the strengths of these programs for prototyping:

- **Learning curve.** PowerPoint and Keynote are perfect for the technically challenged. The applications employ a drag-and-drop model and don't require any coding to create interactivity.

- **Familiarity and presence.** Probably the biggest advantage of PowerPoint is its sheer presence—it's everywhere. Just about every computer on the planet, Mac or Windows, has a copy of PowerPoint or Keynote installed on it. Chances are, you already have the application and so does your intended audience. If your audience doesn't have PowerPoint or Keynote, both programs can export to PDF or HTML.

- **Master slides.** You can use master slides to create templates and share common elements across multiple slides. Master slides also increase productivity and ensure consistency.

- **Copy-and-paste.** You can copy individual elements or entire screens quickly and easily.

- **Rearrange with drag-and-drop.** Rearranging the order of your screens is as simple as dragging-and-dropping. The light table mode displays slides in a grid, making it easy to rearrange entire sections of your prototype.

- **Export to HTML or PDF.** Want to run your prototype in a Web browser? Just export it as HTML. Or export it as a PDF and use Adobe Acrobat to create additional interactivity beyond the capabilities of PowerPoint or Keynote.

Weaknesses

There are a few weaknesses for prototyping with these tools:

- **Limited drawing tools.** The drawing tools in PowerPoint and Keynote are rudimentary. If you want to create high-fidelity designs, you're going to be better off doing that in a program like Illustrator, Fireworks, or Photoshop.

- **Limited interactivity.** Interactivity is limited to hyperlinks. Hyperlinks can only be used to link to other screens within the prototype or URLs.

- **Nonreusable source code.** Neither tool creates reusable source code. Most of the time this isn't an issue because prototypes are typically *not* intended for production. However, in the case where the goal is to create reusable source code, you should consider something else.

In an effort to reduce redundancy, for the rest of this chapter, I'm going to reference *PowerPoint* instead of PowerPoint and Keynote. You can assume that the technique I provide applies to both PowerPoint and Keynote, unless otherwise stated. In the event the same technique doesn't apply, I'll provide a separate Keynote reference.

Creating Narrative Prototypes with PowerPoint

Narrative prototypes are often used to get high-level feedback on things like the basic application flow, or to evaluate the visual aesthetics of a system.

I've used this method in the past to test linear systems, such as mobile or digital video recorders (DVRs). I've also used this method to perform A/B testing on multiple visual designs, which you can read more about in Chapter 12, "Testing Your Prototypes."

Creating a narrative walkthrough or a linear prototype in PowerPoint is pretty straightforward. If you've created your screens in another visual design tool like Photoshop or Fireworks, you simply import the screens in the order you want to display them and that's it. Just run the presentation and click through the slides.

There are no fancy methods, techniques, coding, or adjustments necessary. PowerPoint's default settings are good enough to provide a narrative prototype of screens you designed in another application. You can download a sample prototyping kit for PowerPoint and Keynote at 🎞 rosenfeldmedia.com/books/downloads/prototyping/chapter7.zip.

If, on the other hand, you want to use PowerPoint to create the prototype screens, then there are three basic steps:

Step 1: Set Up Your File

1. Start with a blank screen template by selecting File › New from the application menu.

2. Use Visio, Illustrator, or your favorite drawing program to create a generic window or use a screen grab from your Web browser.

3. Select a master slide and use the generic window as the background for that master.

4. Repeat the third step to create master slides for each of the different template screens you need.

Step 2: Apply a Background Image to a Master Slide in PowerPoint

1. With the master slide selected, right-click on the master slide and select Fill Effects and then Picture and select the picture.

Step 2 (Alternate): Apply a Background Image to a Master Slide in Keynote

1. With the master slide selected, select the Appearance option from the Slide Inspector and then select Background and Image Fill, as shown in Figure 7.2.

FIGURE 7.2
Use a background image on a master slide in Keynote.

Step 3: Create a Set of Common GUI Widgets

Visio, OmniGraffle, Fireworks, and Illustrator all have GUI libraries available, which you can find on the book site. One of the easiest ways to create a common GUI library for PowerPoint is to copy and paste them from one of these existing libraries.

While you can use the basic shape tools in PowerPoint to create GUI widgets, I wouldn't recommend it because they tend to be a bit rudimentary and sloppy in my opinion. Additionally, since there's probably a library readily available for your illustration tool of choice, there's very little reason to create your own.

If you're looking for a set of GUI widgets already created for PowerPoint, you can use the PowerPoint Prototyping Toolkit, which is available at **istartedsomething.com**. The PowerPoint prototyping kit is a collection of application windows, dialog windows, and common GUI controls based on Windows Vista (see Figure 7.3).

TIP GUI MASTER

Create a master slide and use it as your GUI widget palette. Whenever you need a GUI widget, you can copy it from your GUI palette master slide.

FIGURE 7.3
PowerPoint prototyping toolkit.

Creating Interactive Prototypes with PowerPoint

PowerPoint is probably one of the easiest tools for creating basic interactivity. If you can click a mouse, you can create interactive PowerPoint prototypes. You just need to add a few things to your basic narrative prototype:

- Create your keyframes or beginning-and-end states.

- Give your slides meaningful names.

- Add hyperlinks to your buttons.

Step 1: Create Your Keyframes

Keyframes represent the main starting and stopping points in your prototype simulation. For a search-results scenario, you might have a few keyframes: the initial search input screen, the search results display screen, and the individual screen a participant would come to if he/she selected one of the search result items.

When using PowerPoint, keep each keyframe on its own slide. This keeps the prototype simple and makes the screens or states easier to link to. If you forget a few keyframes, don't sweat it. You can always add them later and reorder them using drag-and-drop.

Step 2: Disable Slide on Mouse Click (PowerPoint Only)

1.   From the Slide Show menu, select Slide Transition.

2.   The Advance Slide on Mouse Click is enabled by default, as shown in Figure 7.4. Unselect this option and apply to all.

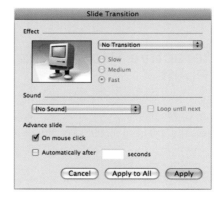

FIGURE 7.4
Disable Advance Slide on Mouse Click in PowerPoint.

A quick warning about hyperlinks in PowerPoint. PowerPoint *doesn't* support hyperlinks on 100 percent transparent objects. Why does this matter? Well, one common method is to use PowerPoint to create interactivity between a series of imported images like visual design comps or screen captures.

Let's take the example of prototyping the Slide Transition screen shown in Figure 7.4. There are a number of actions on this screen, including Cancel, Apply to All, and Apply. Rather than create new buttons for each of these, I'm probably going to just draw a shape around each of the three buttons, make it transparent, and apply an action or hyperlink to go to another screen.

If the shape is 100 percent transparent, PowerPoint won't let you attach a hyperlink to it. The workaround is to give the object an opacity of one percent, and the problem is solved.

TIP ONE PERCENT

If you're using PowerPoint, make sure that your button objects have an opacity of at least one percent in order to hyperlink them.

Step 3: Add Interaction and Hyperlinks to Your Buttons (PowerPoint)

1. To add interaction, select the button and right-click. Then select Action Settings from the menu, as shown in Figure 7.5.

2. Select the Hyperlink To option and pick either Slide or URL, as shown in Figure 7.6.

TIP NAME IT

Give your slides meaningful names. It's much easier to link to the correct slide if it's named Product Details than Slide 41.

FIGURE 7.5
Right-click the menu to select hyperlink in PowerPoint.

FIGURE 7.6
Add interaction on mouse click or mouseover in PowerPoint.

Step 3: Add Interaction and Hyperlinks to Your Buttons (Keynote)

1. Select the Hyperlink Panel in the Inspector.

2. Select the Enable as Hyperlink option and pick either the Slide or URL option (see Figure 7.7).

After you've enabled the button as a hyperlink, you should see a visual cue like the arrow in the blue circle in Figure 7.8.

FIGURE 7.7
Add interactivity to Keynote slides.

FIGURE 7.8
Example of button with interactivity or hyperlink enabled.

That's it. Now you have an interactive prototype. See how easy that is?

AJAX Effects in PowerPoint

The built-in transition effects in PowerPoint make simulating a number of common AJAX effects easy. Let's look at the JavaScript fade technique as an example. This technique is used to highlight the background of an object on the screen for a few quick seconds. After a few seconds, the background color fades out, and the highlight is removed.

This is probably the easiest effect to simulate in PowerPoint.

1. Create two keyframe slides—one that shows the highlight (see Figure 7.9) and one with the highlight removed (see Figure 7.10).

2. Start with the slide that shows the highlight and select the Transition option; then select Dissolve and set the transition to start on the mouse click. Set the delay to one second.

The keyframe with the highlight will fade away and reveal the screen without the highlight, simulating the JavaScript fade technique.

FIGURE 7.9
Keyframe with highlight for JavaScript fade technique.

FIGURE 7.10
Keyframe without highlight for JavaScript fade technique.

You can also apply action effects like Move, Opacity, or Scale to objects in PowerPoint. I've used these effects in the past to simulate other AJAX effects to show and hide objects on the screen.

So even if you can't program AJAX transitions, you can fake them with PowerPoint.

Summary

Okay, here's a quick recap on reasons you might want to consider using PowerPoint or Keynote next time you're prototyping:

- You probably already have it installed.

- The learning curve is pretty low.

- Master slides are great for consistency and efficiency.

- You can export to a clickable PDF or HTML prototype.

Visio

Prototyping Models

Paper... ●
Digital.. ◐
Narrative... ●
Interactive.. ◐
Rapid... ●

Stages

Early... ●
Late.. ◐

Compatibility & Cost

Mac.. N/A
Windows.. ●
Cost.. $129-559

Portability & Use

Web.. ●
Mobile... ◐
Gestural.. ○
Reusable Code.. ○

Collaboration, Distribution, & Traceability

Collaboration.. ◐
Distribution.. ◐
Traceability.. ●

HOW TO READ THIS TABLE

● Ideal   ◐ Capable, but Not Ideal   ○ Not Suitable

Visio

FIGURE 8.1
Flickr Uploadr recreated using Visio 2007 Professional.

I f you've ever worked in a windows environment, chances are you've used Visio. Don't let its roots as a diagramming tool fool you, because Visio can be a useful prototyping tool.

Visio has a fairly low learning curve. If you can drag-and-drop objects onto a page, you can create interfaces for Web-based or desktop systems using Visio. Visio ships with a number of standard shapes, stencils, and templates, which makes creating interfaces faster and easier. If the built-in stencils and templates don't meet your needs, a host of third-party stencils, templates, and prototyping toolkits are just an Internet search away.

In this chapter, we'll explore prototyping with Visio's built-in capabilities, as well as a number of popular third-party stencil and toolkit libraries. You can find a list of these third-party add-ons with links at the end of this chapter.

Strengths

While Visio might not immediately come to mind when you think of prototyping tools, here are a few things that make it worth considering:

- **Learning curve.** Visio uses an object-based drag-and-drop model to create drawings, which creates a relatively low learning curve.

- **Familiarity and presence.** Visio is a common tool for business and technology professionals working in a Windows environment. If your computer has Windows and you're in a corporate environment, chances are you already have Visio.

- **Backgrounds.** Visio supports the use of backgrounds, which can be used to distribute common elements across multiple screens.

- **Stencils, shapes, and templates galore.** Visio ships with a number of stencils, shapes, and templates for creating everything from network diagrams to Windows application interfaces. If the built-in stencils and templates aren't enough, there are a number of solutions created by Bill Scott, Jacco Nieuwland, Nick Finck, Garrett Dimon, and others, which you'll find listed at the end of this chapter.

- **Export to HTML or PDF.** If your audience doesn't have Visio, you can always export the file to HTML or PDF.

- **Programmability.** If you're comfortable with Visual Basic, you can simulate some level of rich interactivity with Visio.

Weaknesses

While good for basic prototyping, Visio has a number of disadvantages that limit its effectiveness as a prototyping tool:

- **Windows only.** Visio doesn't run natively on a Mac. If you're on a Mac, it's probably not an option for creating prototypes. You could run virtualization software to run Windows so you could use Visio, but what's the point? There are a number of other great alternatives.

- **Limited interactivity.** Interactivity is essentially limited to hyperlinks. Hyperlinks can only be used to link to other screens within the prototype or URLs.

- **Limited rich interactivity.** While it is possible to simulate some level of rich interactivity using Visual Basic with Visio, this is beyond the capability and comfort level of most Visio users.

- **Links on backgrounds break when exported.** Links placed on backgrounds are not supported when exporting your prototype as HTML or PDF. If you want that global navigation to work when you export your prototype to HTML or PDF, you'll need to place it on every screen or create invisible elements and link them—which kind of defeats the purpose of a background. This is a major drag.

- **Awkward menus and interface.** Visio can be rather awkward and unintuitive to navigate at times. Several key actions, like the ability to add a hyperlink to an object, are not available via right-click, but only from the main application menu. If you want to access the Shapes menus, you'll need to select File from the main application menu— actually, View or Tools would make more sense. Navigating a 20-plus-page document is downright clunky. Try doing that using the tabs as pages metaphor—it just feels wrong.

- **Nonreusable source code.** When Visio exports to HTML, it creates an image for the entire page and creates image maps for the hyperlinks. The resulting pages are essentially screen captures.

Prototyping with Visio

Visio ships with a number of useful default templates for creating everything from flow diagrams and UML documents to Windows XP user interfaces. For the example in this chapter, we're going to re-create the Flickr Uploadr application—a photo upload utility for the popular Flickr photo site by Yahoo! You can download the sample Visio file used for this chapter at ♠ rosenfeldmedia.com/books/downloads/prototyping/ Visio_Demo.vsd.

Step 1: Create a New File

1. Start by creating a new file by selecting File › New from the application menu. As you can see in the New File menu shown in Figure 8.2, there are a number of useful options that ship with Visio.

2. Selecting New Drawing will create a new blank drawing with access to the default shapes and stencils. Choose New Drawing from Template to use one of your own custom templates. Or select one of the useful templates that ships with Visio from the list of folders displayed in the menu.

3. Selecting one of the templates will load the appropriate shapes and stencils for that drawing automatically.

In this case, we'll choose the Windows XP User Interface from the Software and Database option, as shown in Figure 8.3.

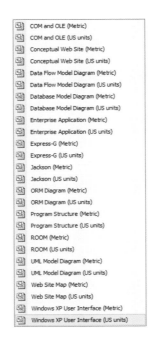

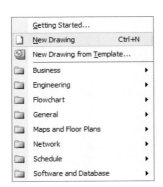

FIGURE 8.2
New File menu in Visio.

FIGURE 8.3
Windows XP User Interface option from the New Drawing menu.

By selecting Windows XP User Interface, we automatically have access to a number of Windows UI shapes and stencils. By default, these will be displayed in the Shapes panel at the left, as shown in Figure 8.4.

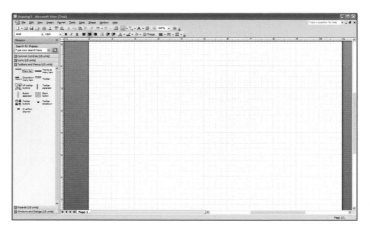

FIGURE 8.4
Shapes panel for displaying Windows and Dialogs shapes in Visio.

Step 2: Create a Basic Application Window

1. Drag a blank window shape from the Windows and Dialogs panel onto the canvas.

2. Add a number of common elements and controls, such as the Status Bar, Menu Bar, and window controls like Minimize, Maximize, and Close. The result should look similar to Figure 8.5.

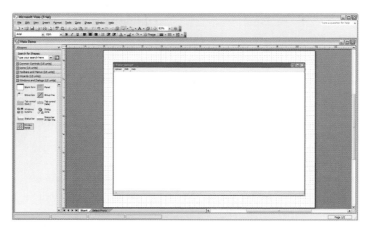

FIGURE 8.5
Drawing of a basic application window in Visio.

At this point, you have a couple of productivity options. You can create a page background or a stencil from your application window drawing.

- **Page Backgrounds.** Can be applied to new pages and are useful for global elements like a container window or navigation menus. Page backgrounds cannot be modified at the page level. Instead, you must modify the original page background drawing.

- **Stencils.** Can be used to define common elements you want to reuse in your document. Stencils can be modified on the page level. Modifications to stencils placed on a page do not affect the original stencil.

For this demonstration, we'll create a stencil first and then apply it to a page background. This gives us the capability to actually create a number of alternate state page backgrounds from the same stencil.

> **TIP** SHOULD I STENCIL OR USE PAGE BACKGROUND?
>
> To create stencils for common elements, you may need to re-size or edit on a page-by-page basis. Create page backgrounds for common elements that you *do* want to apply to multiple pages, but *don't* need to modify on a page-by-page basis.

Step 3: Create a Stencil

1. Start by grouping your drawing. Select all the elements in the drawing and right-click. Select Shape > Group from the menu, as shown in Figure 8.6.

2. After you have your shape grouped, you'll want to save it as a stencil by selecting File > Shapes > New Stencil from the main application menu (see Figure 8.7). Your new stencil will show up in the Shapes menu at the left of your application window.

FIGURE 8.6
Group Shape menu
option in Visio.

FIGURE 8.7
New Stencil menu
option in Visio.

3. Drag your shape to the newly created stencil. You'll now be able to drag this shape from your stencil anytime you need it.

4. Drag any additional shapes you want to reuse to your stencil.

Step 4: Create a Page Background

1. Select one of the current page tabs and right-click it. Select Insert Page from the menu.

2. The Page Properties tab will be selected automatically. The first option is Type. You'll need to select the Background radio button option (see Figure 8.8).

3. Give the page a meaningful name. Meaningful names will help when you're applying backgrounds to future pages, or when you're trying to select the page to link to when you're creating interactivity between pages. In this case, we'll type **Main Application Window**.

4. Apply your application window stencil to the page by dragging it from the Stencil menu onto the canvas area of your drawing.

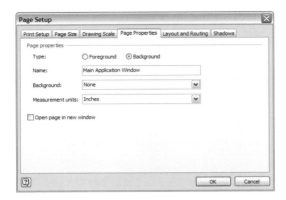

FIGURE 8.8
Set the Page Property
to Background in Visio.

Step 5: Apply a Page Background

1. Select one of the current page tabs and right-click it. Select Insert Page from the menu.

2. The Page Properties tab will be selected automatically. This time, choose Foreground for page type.

3. Give the page a meaningful name. In this case, we'll type **Browse for File**.

4. Click the menu next to Background and select the Main Application Window option, as shown in Figure 8.9. This will apply our main Application Window Background to the new page.

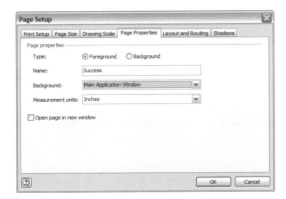

FIGURE 8.9
Apply the Main
Application Window
Background to a new
page in Visio.

Repeat step five to create all the keyframes for your prototype. If you need to create unique page backgrounds, then repeat steps three through five for each.

Now that you have the keyframes, you'll want to make them interactive.

Step 6: Creating Interactivity

1. Select the object you want to link. In this case, we'll choose the Add button.

2. From the main application menu, select Insert › Hyperlink.

3. Choose Address from the dialog window to link to a local file or URL (see Figure 8.10). Choose Sub-address to link to a page within your current drawing. In this case, we'll choose Sub-address.

4. Choose the page you want to link to from the Page menu, as shown in Figure 8.11.

Now you're ready to present your prototype. Presenting your Visio is as easy as selecting View › Full Screen from the main application menu. Alternatively, you can export your Visio file to HTML or PDF for viewing.

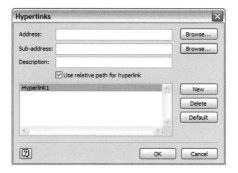

FIGURE 8.10
Hyperlink dialog window in Visio.

FIGURE 8.11
Hyperlink Sub-address dialog window in Visio.

Additional Resources

While Visio does ship with a number of very useful shapes, stencils, and templates, they might not suit your prototyping needs. Thankfully, a number of people have created additional libraries and made them freely available on the Internet.

Swipr

Swipr is an interactive toolkit for Visio developed by Jacco Nieuwland. More information is available at the Swipr Web site at www.swipr.com.

Bill Scott's Prototyping Toolkit for Visio

Bill Scott, the director of UI engineering at Netflix, has created a wireframe prototyping toolkit for Visio and made it freely available. The toolkit includes a number of great features, including the following:

- Complete Web component stencil library (including standard components, table, menus, tabs, and tree)

- Fast, intelligent snap-to layout using preprogrammed Visio connectors

- A way to visualize rich interactions (animating a wireframe)

- Intelligent components that have built-in behaviors

- Generate requirements documents from wireframe artifacts

- Generate code from wireframe artifacts

- Automated annotations and callouts

Bill's prototyping toolkit is available free of charge from his Web site at looksgoodworkswell.blogspot.com/2005/11/visio-wireframe-toolkit-for-download.html.

GUUUI Prototyping Toolkit for Visio

Another good prototyping toolkit for Visio was created by Henrik Olsen. This toolkit includes both a traditional Visio line art template and one that resembles hand-drawn sketches.

Henrick also has a number of articles on using Visio for prototyping. You can find the most recent version of his Visio prototyping toolkit and the related article on his Web site at www.guuui.com/issues/02_07.php.

Nick Finck's Stencil Library

Here is a stencil library for common interface elements like navigation bars, tabs, and links. Nick's stencil library is available free of charge from his Web site at nickfinck.com/stencils.

Garrett Dimon's Templates & Stencils for Visio

Garrett offers a number of templates and stencils for Visio. Need to change the state of a check box or radio button from selected to unselected? Garret's got you covered. Just right-click a check box or radio button, and you can specify whether to show it as selected, checked, enabled, or disabled.See the Web site v1.garrettdimon.com/resources/templates-stencils-for-visio-omnigraffle.

Articles

"Creating an Interactive PDF Prototyping with Visio"

Caitlin Gannon has written an article on using Visio to create an interactive PDF prototype. The article is available from her Web site at caitlingannon.com/2008/03/16/how-to-create-an-interactive-pdf-prototype-in-visio/.

"Prototyping and Usability Testing with Visio"

This is a presentation that was given at the annual STC conference by Karen Bachmann and Whitney Quesenbery. The slides are available in PDF format from the STC Web site at www.stc.org/edu/48thConf/files/VisioPrototyping.pdf

Summary

Okay, quick recap on reasons you might want to consider using Visio next time you're prototyping:

- If you're on a company computer with Windows chances are you probably already have it installed.

- The learning curve is pretty low.

- Backgrounds, stencils, and templates are great for consistency and efficiency.

- You can export to a clickable PDF or HTML prototype.

- When the inner Visual Basic geek strikes, you can use it to create some rich interactivity.

Fireworks

Prototyping Models

Paper .... ◐
Digital .... ●
Narrative .... ●
Interactive .... ●
Rapid .... ●

Stages

Early .... ●
Late .... ●

Compatibility & Cost

Mac .... ●
Windows .... ●
Cost $149-299

Portability & Use

Web .... ●
Mobile .... ●
Gestural .... ○
Reusable Code .... ◐

Collaboration, Distribution, & Traceability

Collaboration .... ◐
Distribution .... ●
Traceability .... ◐

HOW TO READ THIS TABLE

● Ideal ◐ Capable, but Not Ideal ○ Not Suitable

CHAPTER 9

Fireworks

FIGURE 9.1
Fireworks CS4 launch screen.

Adobe Fireworks has been a popular tool among Web professionals since its beginning at Macromedia. Those who use it, love it. No, I mean really love it—as in Fireworks fanboy love it.

I always felt a sense of guilt after speaking with these people. After all, if it was such an amazing tool, why wasn't I using it? Clearly, I was missing out on something.

What drives their dedication and devotion to Fireworks? Many Fireworks fans say it's the ability to create vector and raster artwork with the same tool—it's like having a hybrid of Illustrator and Photoshop, but without all the fat. Others latch onto the image optimization.

With the release of Fireworks CS4, they have one more reason. Fireworks is on its way to becoming a powerful prototyping tool.

Strengths

Fireworks has a long list of features that make it a particularly powerful prototyping tool.

- **Integration improves productivity.** Fireworks integrates exceptionally well with Illustrator, Photoshop, Dreamweaver, Flash, and Device Central. Fireworks maintains Illustrator and Photoshop layers when importing AI and PSD files. Fireworks prototype files can be exported easily as Flash and Photoshop files. Additionally, Device Central lets you test your Fireworks prototypes for mobile devices.

- **Small file size.** By default, Fireworks files are 72dpi, which keeps them relatively small.

- **Page states.** Pages can now have states. The States panel allows you to set up the look-and-feel of each state in the application (for example, logged in versus not logged in). However, when you export the PNG, only the active state will be exported.

- **Asynchronous file saving.** You can save one file and work on another one at the same time. Saving a file doesn't hang up the entire application. This is new to CS4.

- **Vector and raster under one roof.** The ability to create vector and raster art with one tool means you won't have to bounce back and forth between Illustrator and Photoshop. Fireworks also lets you apply the same styles to vector or raster images.

- **Export to HTML, PDF, and more.** Fireworks supports a number of export options, including HTML, PDF, Flash, Flex, and AIR.

- **Flexible enough for lo-fi and hi-fi design.** You can create rough lo-fi designs, as well as fully polished ready-for-prime-time hi-fidelity designs with Fireworks.

- **Ships with useful styles and symbols.** Fireworks ships with a number of built-in styles and symbols for common GUI elements. The large development community continually adds to the collection of Fireworks extensions.

- **Master pages, shared layers, symbols for productivity.** Items on master pages display on every page. Shared layers can be used like master pages, but provide the additional flexibility to pick and choose which pages you share common items on. Symbols are used for common individual items (for example, GUI elements, footers), which will be reused throughout your prototype. Updates to master pages, shared layers, and symbols will apply globally to your Fireworks document.

  The biggest difference between master pages and shared layers is that master pages is an all-or-none model. Shared layers, however, lets you share the item on a page-by-page basis. Moving something on a master page or shared layer will move it throughout the prototype.

- **Preview mode.** The preview mode in Fireworks enables you to test your prototype without having to export it.

Weaknesses

While Fireworks is probably one of the best tools currently available for prototyping, it still has room for improvement.

- **Awkward workflow for Photoshop and Illustrator jockeys.** With the release of CS4, Fireworks has a more familiar Adobe look. However, if you're a Photoshop or Illustrator jockey, you'll find the workflow a bit jarring at first because it's significantly different.

- **Gradient banding.** Gradients created in Fireworks aren't as smooth as those created in Photoshop, resulting in a banding effect.

- **Lack of traceability and documentation support.** If you work in a documentation-heavy environment, you will need a supplemental tool to track requirements and traceability of changes to the prototype.

- **Performance suffers with larger, 50–70-page prototypes.** While Adobe has done a tremendous job at improving performance with CS4, Fireworks shows performance issues when you start to hit the 50–70-page mark in your prototypes. The only current workaround is to separate larger prototypes into multiple files.

- **Limit of one master page per document.** Master pages work like templates. Having only one forces you to use the same template for every page in your prototype, rather than being able to define different masters for each section of your prototype (for example, one for product pages and a different one for shopping cart pages).

Prototyping an iPhone Application with Fireworks

Fireworks CS4 ships with a number of useful GUI symbols for creating Mac, Windows, and Web applications, which makes prototyping with Fireworks faster and easier.

However, for this demonstration, we won't be using the included GUI symbols. Rather, we're going to re-create Twitterific, the popular Twitter application for the iPhone. Don't worry, you won't have to create an entire iPhone stencil. You can download the stencil we used for this chapter at ℳ rosenfeldmedia.com/books/downloads/prototyping/iPhone_Stencil_GUI.png. You can also download the finished prototype file at ℳ rosenfeldmedia.com/books/downloads/prototyping/iPhone_Prototype.png.

Step 1: Create a New File

1. Start by creating a new file by selecting File › New from the application menu (see Figure 9.2) or Create New Fireworks Document from the startup panel (see Figure 9.3).

FIGURE 9.2
New File menu in
Fireworks CS4.

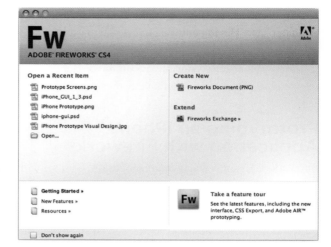

FIGURE 9.3
Create New Fireworks
Document from
Fireworks CS4
startup panel.

2. Enter a width of 320 and a height of 480 on your canvas. This is the default size for iPhone screen applications. The default resolution is 72 pixels/inch (ppi), which will work just fine.

3. Select the canvas background color. White is the default, which should be fine for this example.

Step 2: Create a Master Page

The master page should only hold elements that will carry across all your screens. For this application, we'll need to create a master page with the main toolbar.

1. Add the main toolbar, as shown in Figure 9.4.

2. In the Pages panel (see Figure 9.5), double-click the page name and title it Master.

3. Right-click the page titled Master and select Set As Master Page from the contextual menu (see Figure 9.6).

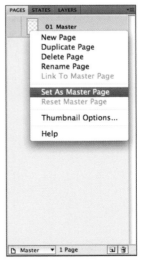

FIGURE 9.4
Main iPhone toolbar.

FIGURE 9.5
Pages panel with
Master page.

FIGURE 9.6
Set As Master Page.

Step 3: Create Key Screens

1. From the Pages panel, right-click the Master Page and select New
   Page. Alternately, you can choose New Page from the Pages panel
   menu, as displayed in Figure 9.7.

2. Double-click the page title in the Pages panel and type Home.

3. Copy the Home screen from one of the iPhone stencils and place it on
   the newly created Home page.

4. Add a Twitterific icon to the Home screen, as shown in Figure 9.8.

5. Repeat steps 1–2 to create the additional screens shown in Figure 9.9.

6. Add the necessary elements to your additional screens.

FIGURE 9.7
New Page from the
Pages panel menu.

FIGURE 9.8
Twitterific icon added to
the Home screen.

FIGURE 9.9
Pages panel displaying
key screens.

TIP SMART NAMES

> Give your pages intelligent names (for example, Home, View
> Message, Reply to Message). When setting up interactivity, it's
> easier to know what Reply to Message is rather than Untitled 3.

Step 4: Add Rollover and Interactivity to Application Icon

1. In the Pages panel, select the Home page.

2. Select the States panel.

3. Double-click State 1 and type in **MouseOut.** Similar to pages, you'll
   want to give your states intelligent names.

4. Add a new state, by right-clicking the MouseOut state and select
   Duplicate State from the menu shown in Figure 9.10.

5. Double-click the new state and type in **MouseOver.**

6. Select the MouseOver state and draw a rounded rectangle over the Twitterific icon. Fill the rectangle with white at 30 percent opacity.

7. Select the MouseOut state again from the States panel.

8. Select the Slice tool from the Web tools section of the Tools palette (see Figure 9.11). Draw a rectangular slice around the Twitterific icon. You should see something that resembles Figure 9.12.

FIGURE 9.10
Duplicate State from
the States panel.

FIGURE 9.11
Web tools in the
Tools palette.

FIGURE 9.12
Home screen with slices for Twitterific application icon.

9. Select the slice and right-click. Select the Add Swap Image Behavior option from the menu shown in Figure 9.13.

FIGURE 9.13
Add Swap Image Behavior option from the contextual menu.

10. In the dialog window, select MouseOver (2) from the option labeled State no: and then select OK. This will create a mouseover effect.

11. Select the slice again and click the list from the Link option in the Properties panel. Select Twitter Stream.htm from the Options menu. This creates a link when you export the prototype from the Twitter icon to the list of twitter messages on the Twitter Stream page of the prototype.

12. Preview the mouseover effect by selecting the Preview button in the top-left corner of the document window. Move your mouse over the Twitter icon, and you should see an opaque effect.

13. Click Original in the top-left corner of the document window to return to editing mode.

Step 5: Add Interactivity to Twitter Stream Screen

1. In the Pages panel, select the Twitter Stream page.

2. Select the Rectangular Hotspot tool from the Web tools section of the Tools palette.

3. Draw a rectangle around the Chat bubble in the toolbar, as shown in Figure 9.14.

FIGURE 9.14

Hotspot created for the Chat bubble.

4. Select the hotspot and then click the List menu from the Link option in the Properties panel. Select the Create New Message.htm option from the menu.

Step 6: Add Interactivity to New Message Screen

1. In the Pages panel, select the Create New Message page.

2. Select the Rectangular Hotspot tool from the Web tools section of the Tools palette.

3. Draw a rectangle around each one of the letter keys on the keyboard and the Close button (see Figure 9.15).

FIGURE 9.15
Hotspots for keyboard letters and Close button.

4. Select one of the letter hotspots and then click the List menu from the Link option in the Properties panel. Select the Type Message.htm option from the menu. Repeat for all the letters.

5. Select the hotspot for the Close button and then click the List menu from the Link option in the Properties panel. Select the Twitter Stream. htm option from the menu.

Step 7: Add Interactivity to Type Message Screen

1. In the Pages panel, select the Type Message page.

2. Select the Rectangular Hotspot tool from the Web tools section of the Tools palette.

3. Draw a rectangle around the Close, Send, and Backspace buttons on the keyboard, as shown in Figure 9.16.

FIGURE 9.16
Hotspots for Close,
Send, and Backspace
buttons on keyboard.

4. Select the Close hotspot and then click the List menu from the Link option in the Properties panel. Select the Twitter Stream.htm option from the menu. Repeat for the Send hotspot.

5. Select the hotspot for the Delete button and then click the List menu from the Link option in the Properties panel. Select the Create New Message.htm option from the menu.

Step 8: Export and Test

1.   Choose Export from the application File menu.

2.   Select a destination folder for your prototype.

3.   Select HTML & Images from the Export option (see Figure 9.17).

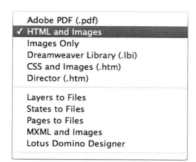

FIGURE 9.17

Export as HTML & Images dialog window.

4.   Select Export Slices from the Slices option. If you don't, the mouseover effect for the Twitter icon won't work.

5.   Deselect Current Page Only. If you don't, you will only get the page currently selected in the Page panel instead of the entire prototype.

6.   Select the Put Images in Subfolder option. This keeps the prototype a little cleaner, placing HTML files in the parent folder and images in an image subfolder.

7.   Press the Export button.

8.   Find the destination folder and open the Home.htm page (or whatever you titled the first screen for your prototype). Double-click it to open it in your Web browser and test your prototype.

9.   Another option is to export your prototype as an interactive PDF. Follow the same instructions as above, but select PDF from the Export option instead of HTML & Images. You'll probably want to change the image compression to JPEG instead of the default JPEG2000, as my JPEG2000 comes out bitmapped.

That's it for this chapter. We've really only scratched the surface of Fireworks as a powerful prototyping tool. I'm sure you're eager to explore Fireworks and see how far you can take it as a prototyping tool.

Additional Resources

So here are a number of additional resources to keep you busy, including iPhone stencils, articles, presentations, and a few videos.

Fireworks Tutorials

Tutorials on just about every aspect of Fireworks from how to get the most out of Master pages to improving your workflow can be found at www. fireworkszone.com.

"Creating an Interactive PDF File from a Multipage Document in Fireworks CS4"

In this article, we'll take a look at how effortless it is to export a PDF from Fireworks, with a focus on creating interactive PDF files. www.adobe. com/devnet/fireworks/articles/interactive_pdf.html

"Designing Interactive Products with Fireworks"

An article by Cooper interactive on how they use Fireworks to design interactive products. www.adobe.com/devnet/fireworks/articles/ cooper_interactive.html

"Fireworks Tips & Tricks—Creating Interactive Prototypes"

David Hogue, Director of Information Design & Usability at Fluid, explains how they use Fireworks for interactive prototypes. tv.adobe.com/#vi+f1498v1660

"Learn Fireworks CS4—Creating Interactive Prototypes for Review"

An overview of the flexible export options supported by Fireworks CS4 from lynda.com. The video covers exporting to HTML, PDF, and even Adobe AIR. tv.adobe.com/#vi+f1594v1015

"Prototyping Adobe AIR Applications with Fireworks CS 4"

A presentation giving a brief overview of prototyping AIR applications using Fireworks CS4. scalenine.com/blog/2008/12/01/adobe-max-presentation-and-source/

"Designing for Mobile Devices Using Fireworks CS4"

A short article outlining some of the techniques used to build the layout and generate the design assets in the mobile application. www.adobe.com/devnet/fireworks/articles/design_mobile_devices_03.html

iPhone GUI Stencils

iPhone Stencil by Teehan+Lax www.teehanlax.com/blog/?p=447

iPhone Icon Template by Keep the Web Weird www.keepthewebweird.com/iphone-icon-psd-template/

iPhone Stencil by 320480 320480.com/

Summary

There's a reason Fireworks has such a strong fan base as a prototyping tool. Here's a few reasons you might want to consider using Fireworks next time you're prototyping:

- It's like Photoshop and Illustrator had a baby—the best of both worlds under one roof.

- It uses master pages, shared layers, and symbols for consistency and efficiency.

- It ships with a number of useful GUI sets.

- You can export to a clickable PDF, HTML, Flash, Flex, and AIR prototype. How's that for flexibility?

- Integration with the rest of the CS suite creates better workflows.

Axure RP Pro

Prototyping Models

Paper	◑
Digital	●
Narrative	●
Interactive	●
Rapid	●

Stages

Early	●
Late	●

Compatibility & Cost

Mac	N/A
Windows	●
Cost	$599

Portability & Use

Web	●
Mobile	◑
Gestural	○
Reusable Code	○

Collaboration, Distribution, & Traceability

Collaboration	◑
Distribution	●
Traceability	●

HOW TO READ THIS TABLE

● Ideal   ◑ Capable, but Not Ideal   ○ Not Suitable

Axure RP Pro

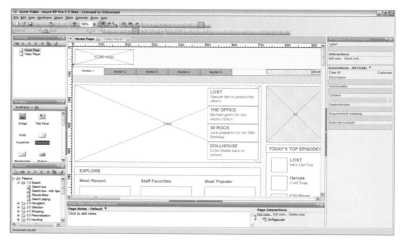

FIGURE 10.1
Acme Video site created using Axure RP 5.5.

I f you created a mash-up between Visio, Word, and Flash lite, you'd get Axure RP—a unified environment for creating wireframes, prototypes, and specifications.

While I hesitate to say that Axure is taking the user experience profession by storm, it's definitely making its mark. With the release of version 5.5, creating highly interactive prototypes is almost effortless.

In this chapter, we'll create an interactive prototype for a video site similar to YouTube or Vimeo. You'll see how easy it is to create advanced interactions, like creating interactive overlays with dynamic panels. At the end of this chapter, you'll find additional resources, including a third-party pattern library with built-in components for navigation, forms, and even a video player.

Strengths

Axure RP Pro has a number of strengths that make it a great prototyping tool:

- **Wireframes, prototypes, and specifications.** Axure lets you use one tool for all your design and documentation needs. The diagramming tools are similar to Visio or OmniGraffle. The real power in Axure, however, is its ability to annotate your designs and automatically generate a specification document and interactive prototype.

- **Low learning curve.** Axure uses an object-based drag-and-drop model to create drawings, similar to Visio and OmniGraffle. Basic interactivity is fairly easy to grasp.

- **Familiarity.** If you've ever used Visio or OmniGraffle, you'll find it relatively easy moving around in Axure. The application has a very similar feel to Visio, but with a better page navigation model, similar to OmniGraffle.

- **Masters and widgets.** Axure ships with a number of widgets for creating common wireframe and flow documents. If those aren't enough for you, there are a number of additional libraries available from their site, or you can create your own.

- **Create interactions without programming.** Axure uses a wizard-like approach to creating interactions. You don't need to know JavaScript to create AJAX-style interactions like overlays, show/hide, or photo carousels.

- **Simple prototype publishing.** When your design is ready, generating a prototype from Axure is as easy as selecting Generate Prototype from the application menu—Axure does the rest.

- **Shared project collaboration.** Axure now makes it easier to work collaboratively on a project. Shared projects give multiple people simultaneous access to the same RP project file. There's even a built-in check-in/check-out system, which includes basic version control.

Weaknesses

While the list is short, Axure RP Pro does have a few shortcomings:

- **Windows only.** Axure doesn't run natively on a Mac. If you're on a Mac, it's probably not an option for creating prototypes. You could run virtualization software to run Windows so you could use Axure, but what's the point? There are a number of other great alternatives like Fireworks, Flash, or HTML.[1]

- **Lack of drawing tools.** Axure lacks basic drawing tools like those found in Illustrator, OmniGraffle, or Visio. Axure does provide shapes you can drag to your page, but if you want to create nice rounded buttons with a gradient effect it's a rather laborious process. You're better off creating them in Photoshop or Fireworks and importing them into Axure.

- **Non-reusable source code.** Axure does generate real HTML pages, as opposed to screen captures with image maps. But nobody in his right mind would use it for production.

Building a Video Web Site Prototype with Axure RP

Axure ships with a number of built-in widgets for creating your prototype designs. You can download the prototype file used for this chapter at

ﯼ rosenfeldmedia.com/books/downloads/prototyping/chapter10.zip.

Step 1: Create a New File

1. Start by creating a new file by selecting File › New from the application menu. By default, Axure will create a new document with a few pages to get you started. You'll see these in the Sitemap panel shown in Figure 10.2.

---

1 Axure for the Mac, aka MAxure, is supposedly in the works according to www.axureformac.com/. At the time of the publication of this book, there was no known release date or license information.

FIGURE 10.2
Sitemap panel.

Step 2: Create the Header

1. f it's not already selected, choose the Wireframe widget set from the
    Widgets panel shown in Figure 10.3.

FIGURE 10.3
Wireframe Widget
panel.

2. Drag the Horizontal Menu element from the Widgets panel to
    the page. Double-click in the center of each element to change the
    text label.

3. Drag a Text Field and Button to the page. Double-click in the center
    of each element to change the text label.

4. The result should look similar to Figure 10.4.

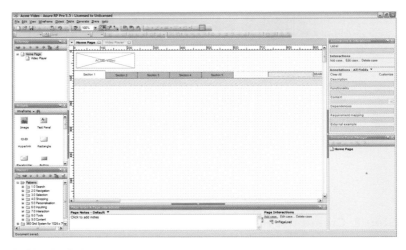

FIGURE 10.4
Example header with navigation and logo.

Step 3: Design the Home Page Content

1. From the Widgets panel, drag Rectangles and Text Panels to the page until you have something that resembles Figure 10.5.

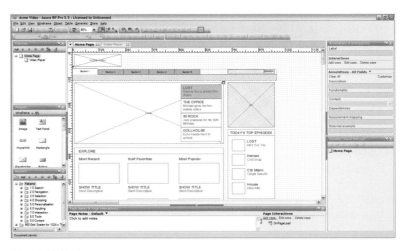

FIGURE 10.5
Example wireframe home page design.

Step 4: Design the Video Player Page Content

1. Select the header elements; then from the application menu, select Edit > Copy.

2. Click the Video Player page; then from the application menu, select Edit > Paste.

3. Drag a Placeholder from the Widgets panel onto the page. You should have something that resembles Figure 10.6.

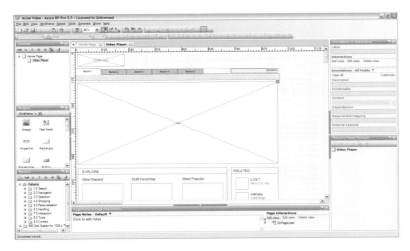

FIGURE 10.6
Example wireframe Video Player content page.

Step 5: Link the Pages

1. Click the Home Page and select the large video placeholder. You should see a green line around the selected item.

2. Make sure that the Annotations & Interactions panel is visible. If it's not, then from the application menu, select View > Annotations & Interactions.

3. From the Annotations & Interactions panel, double-click the OnClick option, as shown in Figure 10.7.

FIGURE 10.7
Annotations &
Interactions panel.

4. The Interactions Case Properties dialog window shown in Figure 10.8 should appear. Enter a meaningful name in the Step 1: Description box (for example, Link to Video Page). Under Step 2: Selection Actions, select the Open Link in Current Window option. Under Step 3: Edit the Actions descriptions, click the Link action.

5. The Link Properties dialog window will appear, prompting you to select a page, as shown in Figure 10.9. Select Video Player from the dialog window and then select OK.

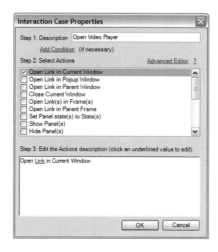

FIGURE 10.8
Interaction Case Properties dialog window.

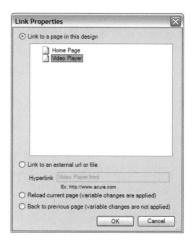

FIGURE 10.9
Link Properties dialog window.

Step 6: Setting up Overlay Effects with Dynamic Panels

1.   Select the Video Player page tab.

2.   Drag two Dynamic Panels from the Widgets panel to the page and
     resize them to fit the video player controls (see Figure 10.10).

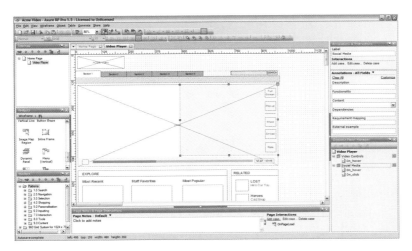

FIGURE 10.10
Example of Dynamic Panels on a screen.

3.   Double-click on Dynamic Panel at the right. The Dynamic Panel State
     Manager dialog window will appear, as shown in Figure 10.11.

FIGURE 10.11
Dynamic Panel State
Manager.

4. Enter a meaningful name in the Dynamic Panel Label field (for example, Social Media Controls).

5. Select the first panel state and select the Rename button. Type **On_hover** in the Name field and select OK.

6. Type a name in the Add new state field, enter On_click, and select OK.

7. From the Dynamic Panel State Manager, select the first state (On_hover) and double-click. A new tab labeled On_hover will appear. A Dynamic Panel Manager panel will also appear on-screen with the On_hover item in bold, as shown in Figure 10.12.

FIGURE 10.12
On-hover Dynamic Panel State Manager.

8. Drag a series of rectangle widgets from the Wireframe panel to your page and give them labels until you have something that looks like Figure 10.13.

9. From the Dynamic Panel Manager panel, select the On_click state and double-click. A new tab labeled On_click (Video Player) will appear.

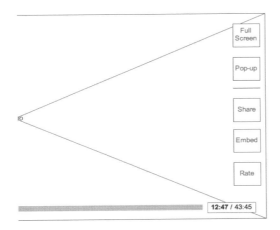

FIGURE 10.13
Social Media Controls
Dynamic Panel.

10. Drag a series of rectangle widgets from the Wireframe panel to your page and give them labels until you have something that looks like Figure 10.14.

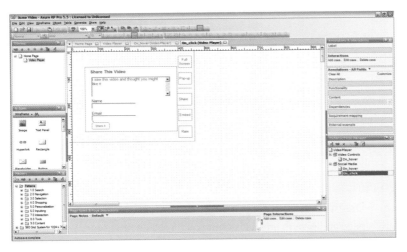

FIGURE 10.14
On_click state of the Social Media Controls Dynamic Panel.

11. From the Dynamic Panel Manager panel, select the On_click state and double-click. A new tab labeled On_click will appear.

12. Select the Share rectangle.

13. In the Annotations & Interactions panel, double-click the On_click option. The Interaction Case Properties dialog window will appear. In Step 1: Description field, enter a meaningful name (for example, Share). In Step 2: Select Actions, select Set Panel state(s) to State(s) from the list of check boxes. In Step 3: Edit Actions description, select the Panel state to State link. A Set Panel state to State dialog window will appear (see Figure 10.15).

14. In Step 1: Select Panels, select the Set Social Media state to State check box. In Step 2: Edit Actions description, select the On hover link. A Select Panel State dialog window will appear, as shown in Figure 10.16.

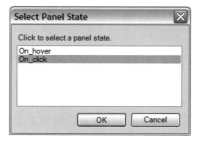

FIGURE 10.15
Set Panel State to State dialog window.

FIGURE 10.16
Select Panel State dialog window.

15. Select the On_click option and then select OK. The dialog window will close revealing the Set Panel state to State window, which should look like Figure 10.17.

16. From the newly updated Set Panel state to State dialog window, select the OK button. This will close the Set Panel state to State dialog window and reveal an updated Interaction Case Properties dialog window (see Figure 10.18).

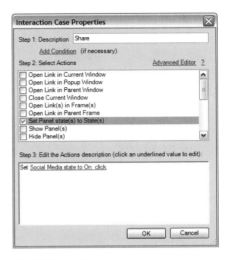

FIGURE 10.17
Updated Set Panel state to State
dialog window.

FIGURE 10.18
Interaction Case Properties dialog
window.

17. From the newly updated Interaction Case Properties dialog window,
     select the OK button.

18. At this point, you can generate your prototype to test the OnClick
     interaction. From the application menu bar, select the Generate item.
     Under Generate, select Prototype (F5), as displayed in Figure 10.19.

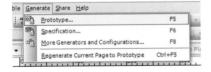

FIGURE 10.19
Generate prototype from
the application menu.

You may notice the hover effects for the dynamic panels are displayed on
the screen as soon as you load the Video Player screen. We'll fix that in
just a second. But first, click the Share item at the right to make sure your
OnClick interaction works correctly.

Step 7: Hiding and Showing Dynamic Panels

By default, Axure shows the first state of a dynamic panel once the page loads. To work around this, you can either create a blank first state or add an interaction to hide the panels on page load.

1. Select the Video Player page tab.

2. In the Page Notes & Interactions panel, select the OnPageLoad option and double-click. The Interaction Case Properties dialog window will appear.

3. In Step 1, enter a meaningful name. In Step 2, Select Hide Panel(s). In Step 3, select the Panel link.

4. In the Select Panels dialog window, select both the Video Controls and Social Media controls options. Then select OK.

5. Select OK from the Interaction Case Properties dialog window.

6. Generate your prototype from the application menu and check to make sure the controls are now hidden.

Step 8: Showing and Hiding Controls on Mouseover

Now that we have the beginning and end states in place, we're going to create the middle states for showing controls when a mouse hovers over the large video player.

1. Select the Video Player page tab.

2. Select the large Video placeholder element on the page.

3. In the Annotations & Interactions panel, select the OnMouseEnter option and double-click. The Interaction Case Properties dialog window will appear.

4. In Step 1, enter a meaningful name (for example, Show Video Controls). In Step 2, Select Show Panel(s). In Step 3, select the Panel link.

5. In the Select Panels dialog window, select both the Video Controls and Social Media controls options. Then select OK.

6. Select OK from the Interaction Case Properties dialog window.

You've just set up the interaction to show controls when the mouse hovers over the Video player placeholder. Now we have to hide them when the mouse leaves the video player placeholder.

1. Select the large Video placeholder element on the page.

2. In the Annotations & Interactions panel, select the OnMouseOut option and double-click. The Interaction Case Properties dialog window will appear.

3. In Step 1, enter a meaningful name (for example, Hide Video Controls). In Step 2, Select Hide Panel(s). In Step 3, select the Panel link.

4. In the Select Panels dialog window, select both the Video Controls and Social Media controls options. Then select OK.

5. Select OK from the Interaction Case Properties dialog window.

At this point, your Annotations & Interactions panel should look like Figure 10.20.

FIGURE 10.20
Example of Dynamic
Panels on a screen.

6. Generate your prototype from the application menu and try it out.

How AnderZorg Learned the Value of Interactive Prototyping

by Henk Wijnholds and Stefan Wobben of Concept7

Concept7 used an interactive prototype as a key communication tool during a redesign process for the AnderZorg (DifferentHealthcare) Web site. The result was a significant improvement in customer satisfaction and online sales.

The unique thing about the Dutch health insurance is that the government obliges insurance companies to offer an obligatory base insurance that covers most common health issues. Beyond that, people can choose additional insurance that covers less common health issues.

The additional insurance options are extremely difficult to compare. They change annually and differ from company to company. In fact, research by Independer.nl (December 9th 2008) says 40 percent of all Dutch health insurance clients don't even know what health care they have, or what exactly is covered.

Our goal was to empower customers with enough information to create a well-informed decision on which insurance to take. We also wanted to make sure to reduce error rates in the subscription flow, making it as easy to use as possible.

To uncover all the pain-points with the current Web site, we performed a combination expert review and eye-tracking study. We found that the old version of the Web site required customers to select an insurance option before they were shown a summary of what it covered.

In one of the studies, we found participants became increasingly frustrated with the lack of information they needed to make their decision. They had to go back and forth between the different insurance options to compare them. The participants had to recall all the information instead of simply recognizing the differences.

We started by creating a lot of idea sketches and hand-drawn screen mock-ups. We thought a matrix would be the best solution to help customers decide between the different insurance options. We used the mock-ups as input for sessions with AnderZorg to prepare their organization and explore possibilities.

How AnderZorg Learned the Value of Interactive Prototyping (continued)

The details define a good or bad customer experience. In this particular case, good content was of extreme importance. By using real content in the interactive prototype, which we've made with Axure RP Pro, we could see how participants reacted to labels and content when visiting the site. This is something we couldn't have tested as effectively without an interactive prototype.

By creating a prototype, we were able to show a matrix version (see Figure 10.21) of the coverage summaries in advance, allowing customers to review information about the different insurance options. During testing, we heard a number of participants make comments like, "Now I can base my decision on something more informed; this is much better."

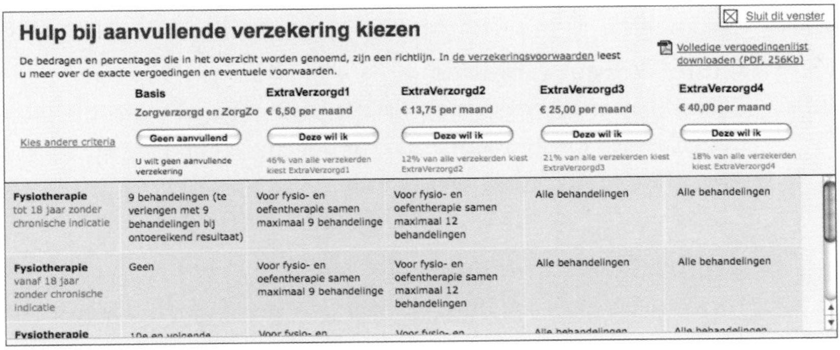

FIGURE 10.21
Prototype of insurance matrix.

A side benefit of the interactive prototype was the benefit to content creators and owners. It helped subject matter experts and content writers see more clearly where their input was required. They learned that interactive prototypes are much more efficient than written documents.

Through the use of a prototype, we were able to increase customer satisfaction from 72 percent to 82 percent. According to independent market research, this is among the highest in the Netherlands, even outside their branch.

The "redesigned" AnderZorg Web site also resulted in an increase of their conversion rate by 48.15 percent, and it doubled the number of subscriptions for health care insurance.

Additional Resources

Axure has a number of video tutorials and add-on libraries available from their Web site. Additionally, some of these third-party resources will make creating advanced AJAX-style interactions much easier.

Axure Video Tutorials

A number of video tutorials are available directly from the Axure Web site at www.axure.com/expert.aspx.

Axure Sample Files

Download sample RP projects and strengthen your prototyping chops from the Axure Web site at www.axure.com/sampleProjects.aspx.

Axure Widget Libraries

Common interface icons and design components based on the YUI! Design Stencil Kit are available directly from the Axure Web site at www.axure.com/widgetLibraries.aspx.

Axure RP Master Library

Thanks to Ian Fenn and Luke Perman, you can get your hands on a component library that makes creating AJAX-style interactions in Axure even easier. The Axure RP Master Library is hosted at Google Code code.google.com/p/axlib/. You can also find them on Twitter @axlib.

Loren Baxter's Axure Design Library

This library includes a number of design patterns for things like AJAX field validation, self-healing, and carousels. You can grab Loren's Axure Design Pattern Library online at www.acleandesign.com/2008/09/axure-design-pattern-library-v2/.

Summary

Axure RP Pro has definitely made its mark on the prototyping scene. Here are a few reasons you might want to consider using Axure RP Pro next time you're prototyping:

- If you know Visio, it's like that, but with more prototyping power.

- You can have one tool for wireframes, specifications, and prototyping.

- You'll have masters and built-in widgets for common GUI elements.

- Generating a clickable HTML prototype is a breeze.

HTML

Prototyping Models

Paper .... ◖
Digital .... ●
Narrative .... ●
Interactive .... ●
Rapid .... ●

Stages

Early .... ●
Late .... ●

Compatibility & Cost

Mac .... ●
Windows .... ●
Cost .... FREE

Portability & Use

Web .... ●
Mobile .... ●
Gestural .... ◖
Reusable Code .... ●

Collaboration, Distribution, & Traceability

Collaboration .... ●
Distribution .... ●
Traceability .... ●

HOW TO READ THIS TABLE
● Ideal   ◖ Capable, but Not Ideal   ○ Not Suitable

CHAPTER 11

HTML

FIGURE 11.1
Source code window of HTML prototype.

HTML prototypes can be a number of different things from slap-and-map to production level simulations.

The slap-and-map method uses HTML to slap together a few JPG images and uses image maps to create interactivity.

Throw-away HTML prototypes do rely on HTML as the underlying source code, but cannot, or should not, be reused for production. An example of this can be seen in the prototype output from Axure RP Pro or by using an editor like Dreamweaver in WYSIWYG mode.

And then there is the production level HTML prototype—the Holy Grail of prototyping methods. Well, that is, if you are comfortable hand-coding HTML. This is currently the least common, but my preferred HTML prototyping method.

The introduction of CSS frameworks including Blueprint, 960, and YUI! combined with popular JavaScript frameworks including jQuery, Prototype, and YUI! (yes, they have both a CSS and JavaScript framework) have made HTML prototyping even easier.

If you're willing to roll up your sleeves and get your hands dirty, I think you'll find HTML prototyping easier than you expect. You just have to get past that initial fear and intimidation factor. Consider reading this chapter as your first step.

Strengths

Some of the strengths that make HTML prototyping the Holy Grail include:

- **Platform independent.** You can code HTML on Mac, Windows, or Linux.

- **Free.** There are countless free HTML editors available.

- **Portable.** You can post HTML prototypes on a server and share them with anyone anywhere around the world. They don't need to download anything to view it.

- **It's real.** HTML prototypes are about as close to the real thing as you can get.

- **Gauge feasibility.** Working with real code gives you a better sense of what's possible and how much effort it will take.

- **Modular, component-based.** HTML prototypes can include files that take a modular, component-based approach. As such, productivity and consistency are increased.

- **Lots of free frameworks.** The rise in availability of free frameworks like jQuery, Prototype, and Blueprint have made HTML prototyping more easily accessible than ever before.

- **Collaborative.** Since HTML prototypes aren't based on a single file, multiple team members can work on the prototype at once. One word of caution: If more than one person is working on an HTML prototype, use some type of version control like GitHub or Subversion to prevent a heart attack when someone accidentally overwrites a file.

- **Reusable code.** Done correctly, the time and effort invested in the prototype can often be put to use in production. The production level code we create at Messagefirst often provides the engineering team with 80–85 percent of the presentation layer code that is needed for production and implementation.

- **Unlimited potential.** Anything is possible in software, as long as you want to take the time and effort.

Weaknesses

Ah, but nothing is perfect. These few things keep HTML from being the perfect prototyping method:

- **Time and effort.** When you first start out, coding HTML prototypes can be time consuming. You should expect some initial ramp-up time. After your skill levels improve, most likely you'll be able to create HTML prototypes as fast, if not faster, than you could prototype with other tools.

- **Annotations.** Annotating your HTML prototypes can be challenging. Common approaches include attaching notes at the bottom of each page or including them in a ‹div› that can be toggled on and off. The W3C is also working on a tool to include annotations via RDF.

Prototyping with HTML

I haven't done a wireframe since 2006, and I don't ever intend to do another one—*ever*! I love prototyping with HTML, CSS, and JavaScript. And I think I love it for two reasons.

First, I love the challenge. It's really easy to mock up a few screens in Fireworks and fake the interactivity. There's something about trying to figure out how to code some of the impossible designs we come up with that gives me a natural rush.

I'll admit, it's frustrating dealing with cross-browser issues, especially when it comes to IE6, the bane of every developer's existence. But...

When I see something I've been prototyping come to life, I imagine that scene from the original *Frankenstein* movie where Dr. Henry Frankenstein, played by Colin Clive, raises his hands in the air and shouts "It's alive." Yeah, it's like that.

Second, the reactions I get from clients when showing them HTML prototypes far exceeds anything I've ever seen from other methods. I've literally had clients almost jump out of their chair in excitement upon seeing some AJAX-style effect on-screen.

AJAX-Style Interactions

Not long ago, we were working on designing an internal application for a client. The application was used to set up new projects in their system and notify people assigned to the project.

Being a fan of minimalist design, we decided to use AJAX-style effects, like progressive reveals and self-healing system messages, to keep the screen as clean as possible at all times.

Rather than show all the available options on the screen at once, we would show only the required fields. Once an agent selected a field that had dependent fields, the dependent fields would be progressively revealed on-screen.

After a few steps, the new project would be set up, and the agent would be redirected back to his dashboard screen with a success message at the top of the screen telling him the new project had been set up. After a few seconds, the success message would snap-close, fading away.

When we showed the prototype to the client, the head of the group was only half-engaged in the meeting. He was going back and forth between email on his Blackberry and paying attention to the presentation. That was—until the success message effect.

Just as we completed the project setup, he looked up to see the success message on-screen. Then he saw it slowly snap-close and fade away—*automagically*.

He slammed his blackberry down on the conference room table and shouted "Holy cow! That was the coolest thing I've ever seen. Can you make it do that again?" And so, I did.

I've never received a reaction like that from a client when showing them wireframes. Ever since I've started doing HTML prototypes, seeing clients freak out with excitement has become rather common.

Creating an HTML Prototype

In some cases, the source code you'll find in this chapter is wrapped due to limited width of the printed page. Anytime you see this symbol "↵" it represents a line wrap in the source code. The sample files available from the book's Web site will not have the "↵" symbol in the source code.

Before you start, you may want to download the example files from the book's Web site at ♔ rosenfeldmedia.com/downloads/prototyping/ chapter11.zip). The example files include two additional CSS files used for formatting text and the form elements, as well as an image for the form button, none of which are included in the instructions below.

If you prefer to start from scratch without the example files, the tutorial will still work—it just won't look as pretty.

Step 1: Create a New File

Start with a blank HTML document and save it as index.html. I like to start each of my HTML prototypes with the following:

```
<!DOCTYPE html PUBLIC "-//W3C//DTD HTML 4.01//EN"
    "http://www.w3.org/TR/html4/strict.dtd">
<html lang="en">
<head>
<meta http-equiv="Content-Type" content="text/html; charset=utf-8">
<title>Untitled Document</title>
<!-- Import CSS framework -->
<!-- Import JavaScript framework -->
</head>
<body>
</body>
</html>
```

You might notice a few comment tags. These are placeholders for our CSS and JavaScript frameworks we'll import to make the prototype look nice and add some AJAX-style interactivity.

Step 2: Add Basic Structure

Now that we have the basic HTML document created, we need to create the basic structure that will hold our content. The most common elements include a header, navigation, main content area, sidebar, and footer. We'll start by adding a div container for each of these main content holders.

```
<div class="wrapper">
  <div id="Header"></div>
  <div id="Nav"></div>
  <div id="Main">
    <div id="Sidebar"></div>
  </div>
  <div id="Footer"></div>
</div>
```

TIP MAKE IT EASY TO DISTINGUISH BETWEEN CLASSES AND IDS

When creating CSS styles, I prefer to use a naming convention of lowercase for Classes (for example, wrapper) and Camel-Case for IDs (for example, SlideShow). This makes it easier to scan the source code quickly and distinguish between Class and ID elements.

You might have noticed that I've included a "wrapper" div around the structural elements. This is done to keep all the elements wrapped up in a handy container that is 950 pixels wide and centered in the screen through a little CSS we'll add later.

Now that we have our basic structure in place, let's add some content. We'll start by adding a logo, some navigation, an article section, and heading elements to each of our main containers:

```
<div class="wrapper">
  <div id="Header">
    <div id="Logo">
      <h1>ACME</h1>
    </div>
```

HTML   155

```
    </div>
    <div id="Nav">
      <ul>
        <li class="current"><a href="#">Home</a></li>
        <li><a href="#">About</a></li>
        <li><a href="#">Blog</a></li>
        <li><a href="#">Contact</a></li>
      </ul>
    </div>
    <div id="Main" class="clearfix">
      <div id="Article">
        <div class="container">
          <h2>Content</h2>
        </div>
      </div>
      <div id="Sidebar">
        <div class="container">
          <h2>Sidebar</h2>
        </div>
      </div>
    </div>
    <div id="Footer">
      <div class="container">
        <h2>Footer</h2>
      </div>
    </div>
  </div>
```

At this point, if you open the page in your browser, you'll see something like Figure 11.2.

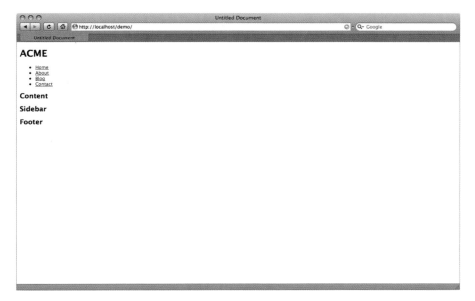

FIGURE 11.2
Basic unstyled HTML prototype.

Step 3: Style the Basic Structural Elements

Now that we have our basic structure in place, we can add some style to the elements. A common issue with designing for the Internet is that each Web browser has its own default settings for rendering HTML elements. Our first order of business will be to fix that. We're going to whip the browsers into shape with the use of a CSS reset.

There are a number of CSS reset files available on the Internet. Two of the most common are available from Eric Meyers (**meyerweb.com/eric/tools/css/reset/**) and Yahoo! (**developer.yahoo.com/yui/reset/**).

1. Create a new file with the following and save it as reset.css:

```
html, body, div, span, object, iframe, h1, h2, h3, h4, h5, h6, ↵
p, blockquote, pre, a, abbr, acronym, address, code, del, dfn, ↵
em, img, q, dl, dt, dd, ol, ul, li,

fieldset, form, label, legend, table, caption, tbody, ↵
tfoot, thead, tr, th, td {margin:0; padding:0; border:0; ↵
font-weight:inherit; font-style:inherit; font-size:100%; ↵
font-family:inherit; vertical-align:baseline;}


body {line-height:1.618;}
table {border-collapse:separate; border-spacing:0;}
caption, th, td {text-align:left; font-weight:normal;}
table, td, th {vertical-align:middle;}


blockquote:before, blockquote:after, q:before, ↵
q:after {content:"";}
blockquote, q {quotes:"" "";}
a img  {border:none;}
```

TIP USING A MODULAR FRAMEWORK APPROACH
TO YOUR HTML PROTOTYPES

I create a single CSS file called "style.css" and use the @import method to include reset.css, typography.css, base.css file, and custom.css files. The reset.css file resets all browsers to the same defaults. The typography.css file sets up the type styles. The base.css file sets up the basic structure (for example, header, logo, navigation, main, sidebar, article, footer) for my prototyping framework. Finally, I use the custom.css file to customize the look-and-feel of the prototype. By taking this approach, I only have to deal with the 30–100 lines of CSS code in the custom.css file to customize the look-and-feel and troubleshoot for cross-browser issues.

We'll skip over the typography.css file I typically use in my prototyping framework, which is included in the downloadable files at 📻 rosenfeldmedia.com/downloads/prototyping/chapter11.zip.

Now that we have all the browsers behaving nicely, we'll create the CSS to style the main elements on the screen.

2. Create a new file with the following code and save it as base.css:

```
body {margin:2px 0; background:#111;} /* Gives the body a ↵
little breathing room up top and on bottom. */

.wrapper {width:950px; margin:0 auto; background:#eee;} ↵
/* Groups everything and centers it on the screen. */


/* Establish basic layout elements.
------------------------------------------------- */
#Header, #Logo, #Search, #Nav, #Main, #Article, ↵
#Section, #Sidebar, #Footer {margin:0; padding:0;}


/* Header elements.
------------------------------------------------- */
#Header {height:48px;}

#Logo {width:230px; padding:5px 10px;}

#Nav {height:30px; width:950px; border-bottom:1px solid #ddd;}


/* Main navigation elements.
------------------------------------------------- */
#Nav ul {margin:10px 0 -9px 10px;}

#Nav li {height:24px; padding:5px 10px; ↵
list-style-type:none; display:inline; color:#4a69a5;}

#Nav li a:link, #Nav li a:visited {color:#0089dc; ↵
text-decoration:none;}

#Nav li a:hover {color:#222;}

#Nav li.current,#Nav li.current a:link ↵
{font-weight:bold; color:#222;}

#Nav li.current a:link {border-bottom:2px solid #222}


/* Main elements.
------------------------------------------------- */
#Main {width:950px; border-bottom:1px solid #ddd; ↵
border-top:1px solid #fff;}

#Article {float:left; margin:0 10px 0 ↵
0;width:670px; min-height:540px; background:#fff;}


/* Sidebar elements.
```

```
--------------------------------------------- */
#Sidebar {float:right; width:270px;}
#Sidebar .container {margin:0 10px 10px 0;}


/* Footer elements.
--------------------------------------------- */
#Footer {height:120px; width:950px; color:#eee; ↵
border-top:1px solid #fff; }


/* Tables
--------------------------------------------- */
th {background:#fff;}
tr td {border-bottom:1px solid #ddd;}
tr.even td {background:#e5ecf9;}
tr.new-comment td {background:#ffffdd;}


/* Miscellaneous elements.
--------------------------------------------- */
.container {padding:1.5em;margin-bottom:1.5em;} /* Use to create a
padded box inside a column.   */

hr{background:#ddd; color:#ddd; clear:both; ↵
float:none; width:100%; height:1px;margin: 1em 0 ↵
1.45em 0; border:none;} /* Use to create a horizontal ↵
ruler across a column. */


/* Clearing floats without extra markup based on ↵
How To Clear Floats without Structural Markup by PiE ↵
[http://www.positioniseverything.net/easyclearing.html] */
.clearfix:after, .container:after {content:" "; ↵
display:block; height:0; clear:both; visibility:hidden;}
.clearfix, .container {display:inline-block;}
* html .clearfix, * html .container {height:1%;}
.clearfix, .container {display:block;}
```

3. Create a new file with the following and save it as style.css:

```
@import 'reset.css';
@import 'base.css';
```

4.   Place the following right after the ‹!-- Import CSS framework --› comment to link the CSS files:

```
<link rel="stylesheet" href="lib/css/style.css" ↵
8 type="text/css" media="screen, projection" />
```

Open the index.html page in your browser (see Figure 11.3).

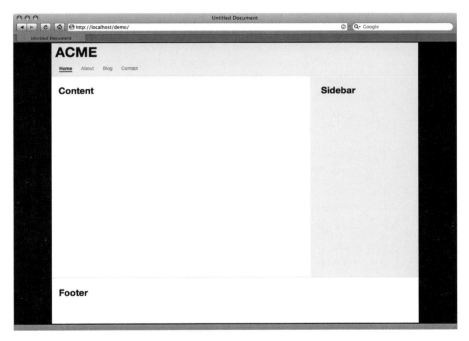

FIGURE 11.3
HTML prototype structure with basic style.

Step 4: Add Some Content

Our basic structure is in place and all we need to do now is add some content. We'll add some lorem ipsum text for a blog entry and then some comments. At the bottom of the comments, we'll create a form to post another comment. Clicking the Post Message button will perform an AJAX-style auto-post on the screen.

1. Add a heading and a few lines of lorem ipsum text inside the Article section:

```
<div id="Article">
 <div class="container">
  <h2>Most Awesome Blog Post Ever</h2>
   <p>Lorem ipsum dolor sit [...].</p>
  </div>
</div>
```

2. After your blog post, add the Comments section. This will include a comment that we'll initially hide using jQuery. The following code has to come after the last line of your blog post, but before the end of the "container" div tag.

```
<hr />
 <h3>Comments</h3>
  <table>
   <tr>
    <th width="25%"></th>
    <th width="75%"></th>
   </tr>
   <tr class="new-comment">
    <td><strong>Tom Sawyer</strong><br />
     <span class="quiet">1 minute ago</span></td>
    <td>Sit amet, consectetuer adipiscing[..].</td>
   </tr>
   <tr>
    <td><strong>Betty Boop</strong><br />
     <span class="quiet">4 minute ago</span></td>
    <td>Lorem ipsum dolor sit amet, con[...].</td>
   </tr>
   <tr>
    <td><strong>Barney Rubble</strong><br />
     <span class="quiet">16 minute ago</span></td>
```

```
    <td>Consectetuer adipiscing elit, [...].</td>
  </tr>
  <tr>
   <td><strong>Winnie Pooh</strong><br />
    <span class="quiet">45 minutes ago</span></td>
   <td>Sed diam nonummy nibh euismod [...].</td>
  </tr>
 </table>
<h3>Say Something</h3>
 <form>
  <ul>
   <li>
    <label for="Name">Name</label>
    <input id="Name" class="third" />
   </li>
   <li>
    <label for="Email">Email</label>
    <input id="Email" class="third" />
   </li>
   <li>
    <label for="Comment">Comment</label>
    <textarea id="Comment"></textarea>
   </li>
   <li>
    <label></label>
    <a href="#" id="PostMessage"><img
    src="images/post-message.gif" /></a></li>
  </ul>
 </form>
```

3. Next, we link the jQuery library in the header just below the Import
    Javascript framework comment tag.

```
<!-- Import JavaScript framework -->
<script src="lib/js/jquery-1.2.6.min.js"></script>
```

4.   Finally, all we need to do is add a little jQuery magic in the header of the HTML page just below the linked jQuery file:

```
<script>
// When the page is ready
  $(document).ready(function(){
    $(".new-comment").hide();


    $("a#PostMessage").click(function () {
    $(".new-comment").show();
  });


  });
</script>
```

That's it. Open your updated prototype in a Web browser, as shown in Figure 11.4.

FIGURE 11.4
Final HTML prototype with blog post and comments.

Click the Post Message button, and you'll see the new comment appear at the top of the comments list with a pale yellow highlight, as seen in Figure 11.5.

FIGURE 11.5
HTML prototype
with new blog post
highlighted.

I like to refer to this AJAX-style transition as a progressive reveal. It's a great technique to use when you have a lot of conditional or interdependent content on a screen (where selecting an item on-screen changes the content for something else on-screen).

In 2008, I used this method in a prototype while redesigning an online application for a university. The existing application process consisted of 13 total screens and took participants no less than 20 minutes to complete. This is the story of how I used the progressive reveal technique to redesign the application process to two screens, which took participants an average of 2.5 minutes to complete.

Case Study: How Prototyping Led to an 85 Percent Reduction in Waste

by Todd Zaki Warfel

In 2008, my company, Messagefirst, was approached to redesign the Web site and online application process for a university. We specialize in increasing conversion rates and improving experiences for transaction-based systems.

While the university's conversion rates were fair, they couldn't help but think they were leaving money on the table and that their application process could be improved.

Whenever we redesign an existing system, we like to do a baseline usability test. A baseline usability study not only allows us to uncover significant problems, but it also provides a key measurement for ROI. The only way to truly measure the ROI success or failure of a design is to measure it against the previous design.

During our baseline test, we found that participants struggled with the existing 13-page application process. The thought of 13 pages was overwhelming and intimidating. Several participants expressed concerns that they might get partially through the process and lose all their information when the browser crashed—an extremely frustrating experience.

We also noticed a significant amount of scrolling and pogo-sticking through the long screens of seemingly endless form fields, many of which didn't apply to their situation. The combination of a 13-page process, scrolling, pogo-sticking, and errors due to unrelated fields resulted in participants averaging around 25 minutes to complete the application process.

Our approach was to take all the current information and fields in the application process and use an AJAX-style progressive reveal method. Each screen would start by displaying only the minimum amount of information necessary to begin and then gradually reveal content and functionality based on a participant's selection.

We hoped the new design would address the following issues:

- **Reduce fear and intimidation.** Rather than be greeted by a screen with 20–30 fields and an indicator they were about to begin a 13-step process, we presented five contact information fields and a visual indicator they were about to start a two-step process.

Case Study: How Prototyping Led to an 85 Percent Reduction in Waste (continued)

- **Prevent errors.** Remove any unrelated fields on-screen. Start only with what's necessary, as shown in Figure 11.6. Don't even give them the chance to make a mistake.

- **Create a cleaner, more readable interface.** Once a selection is made, automatically convert it to readable text instead of populated form fields, and use the progressive reveal technique to show the next option, as shown in Figures 11.7 and 11.8.

- **Provide error recovery.** If they accidentally selected the wrong option, or changed their mind, give them the ability to edit an option in place. Clicking the readable text would swap it out to an editable field.

- **Improve efficiency and satisfaction.** We wanted to get potential students through the application process faster, with fewer errors, and feeling more satisfied with the process.

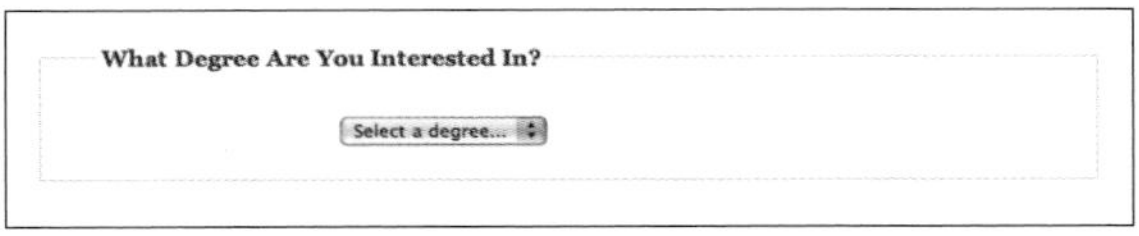

FIGURE 11.6
Select a degree option with progressive reveal.

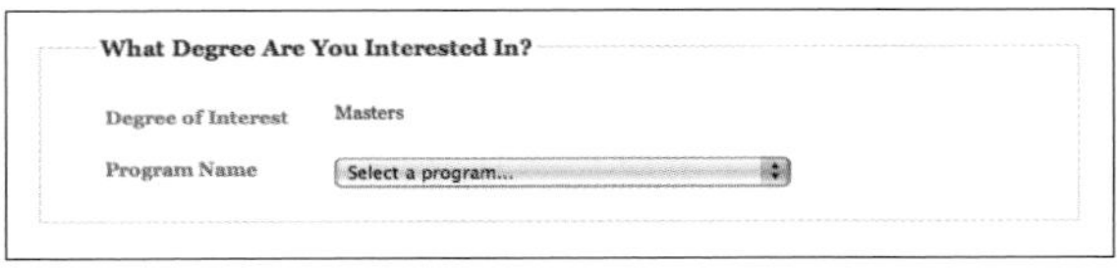

FIGURE 11.7
Select a program option with progressive reveal.

FIGURE 11.8
Select a concentration option with progressive reveal.

How did we do? We were able to keep the same information, but use AJAX-style transitions to reduce 13 pages to two screens—an *85 percent* improvement.

On average, completion times were reduced from 25 minutes to less than 2.5 minutes each—a *1,000 percent* improvement.

Case Study: How Prototyping Led to an 85 Percent Reduction in Waste (continued)

Error rates were also reduced from 2.5 on the original model to zero with the prototype. Participants remarked at how much cleaner the new interface was than the original. Several participants actually got excited when they saw the progressive reveal and commented that they really liked the way that new information was displayed only after a selection was made.

Finally, the overall satisfaction ratings improved from 60 percent to 95 *percent* with the prototype.

A prototype was the only way we could truly convey, test, and measure the impact of our design decisions and the progressive reveal technique.

Additional Resources

Here are some additional resources that might be useful for you.

Tools

Dreamweaver. A Web site and application development environment from Adobe. The split screen and live preview modes give you a rough idea of what your prototype will look like in a browser without ever leaving Dreamweaver. And for those purists, like myself, you don't have to worry about Dreamweaver overwriting your hand-coded HTML. **www.adobe. com/products/dreamweaver/**

TextMate. TextMate brings Apple's approach to operating systems into the world of text editors. By bridging UNIX underpinnings and GUI, TextMate cherry-picks the best of both worlds to the benefit of expert scripters and novice users alike. **macromates.com/**

Coda. A great little "one-window development tool" from the gang over at Panic Software. **www.panic.com/coda/**

Frameworks

960 Grid System. The 960 Grid System is an effort to streamline Web development workflow by providing commonly used dimensions, based on a width of 960 pixels. There are two variants: 12 and 16 columns, which can be used separately or in tandem. 960.gs/

Blueprint. Blueprint is a CSS framework, which aims to cut down on your development time. It gives you a solid foundation to build your project on, with an easy-to-use grid, sensible typography, useful plug-ins, and even a style sheet for printing. www.blueprintcss.org/

jQuery. This is a fast and concise JavaScript Library that simplifies HTML document traversing, event handling, animating, and AJAX interactions for rapid Web development. jQuery is designed to change the way that you write JavaScript. jquery.com/

Prototype. This is a JavaScript framework that aims to ease development of dynamic Web applications. www.prototypejs.org/

Script.aculo.us. Used with Prototype, it provides easy-to-use, cross-browser user interface JavaScript libraries to make your Web sites and Web applications fly. script.aculo.us/

Protonotes. A little JavaScript library that enables you to add Post-it note-style annotations to your prototypes. www.protonotes.com/

Articles

"Just Build It: HTML Prototyping and Agile Development" by Garrett Dimon www.digital-web.com/articles/just_build_it_html_prototyping_and_agile_development/

"HTML Wireframes and Prototypes: All Gain and No Pain" by Julie Stanford www.boxesandarrows.com/view/html_wireframes_and_prototypes_all_gain_and_no_pain

Summary

Sometimes there's just nothing better than the real thing. Take a little time to learn HTML, CSS, and basic JavaScript—it's a whole new world of prototyping. Here are a few reasons you might want to consider using HTML next time you're prototyping:

- It's a lot easier than you think.

- A number of freely available CSS and JavaScript frameworks are available to get you started.

- It's free.

- It's the real deal, which means you're more likely to be able to gauge feasibility and value.

- It's one of the few truly collaborative tools and methods available.

- It opens the possibility to leverage the code for production, saving a significant amount of time to market.

Testing Your Prototype

Testing is often the ultimate goal of prototyping. Even if it's not the ultimate goal, then it should be one of the major milestones along the way.

Usability testing is an entire industry. Usability has its own professional organizations: the UPA (Usability Professionals Organization) and the ACM's SIGCHI. Many books have been written on usability testing, notably *Usability Engineering* by Jakob Nielsen and *A Practical Guide to Usability Testing* by Joseph Dumans and Janice Redish. There's even an entire U.S. government site dedicated to the subject, **usability.gov**.

With all this information readily available, it's a wonder that so many mistakes are commonly made during usability testing. Well, not really. Usability testing isn't one-size-fits-all.

Common Mistakes

There are different methods, such as in-person and remote testing. There are different tools, like Silverback, Morae, or just a simple video camera mounted on a tripod. And there seem to be more ways to run and report a study than Ben & Jerry's flavors of ice cream.

While this chapter won't turn you into a seasoned usability professional overnight (only experience can do that), it will highlight a number of common mistakes and tell you how to avoid them.

Mistake #1: Usability Testing Is a Process, Not an Event

The process of usability testing has a number of equally important pieces, including planning, recruiting, test moderation, analysis, and reporting.

Just sitting someone down in front of a product or service and watching him use it isn't that difficult. Getting quality results from testing, however, that's another story.

Understanding that usability testing is a process and that each piece has an important role to play will go a long way toward improving the quality of your results.

Mistake #2: Poor Planning

When planning your usability test, it's important to understand the who, what, when, where, why, and how of testing.

The first question to ask yourself is: Why are you doing usability testing? Usability testing is great for finding out how something performs, based on measuring time, effort, and satisfaction.

If, on the other hand, you want to get feedback on something less objective or measurable, like whether they like visual design option A better than visual design B, usability testing isn't the best method. This could be something you included at the end of your usability test, but it isn't a reason to choose usability testing as a research method.

Determine whom you want to test. Who uses the product or service? What are their behaviors? Why would they use it in the first place?

Set a testing date and work backward from that. Our usability testing cycle at Messagefirst is typically three to four weeks from initial planning to producing a report. A typical timeline might look something like this:

- **Week 1:** Recruit screener and test scenario development.

- **Week 2:** Recruit participants, finish testing scenarios and prototype.

- **Week 3:** Test prototype and begin analysis.

- **Week 4:** Finish analysis and report findings.

Mistakes in planning often result in underqualified test participants, issues with the prototype, and ultimately poor quality research results. Give yourself enough time to plan properly. It's really that simple.

Mistake #3: Not Recruiting the Right Participants

We have a saying in the field of research: "Bad data in, bad data out." The whole point of usability testing is to see how your design works through the eyes of the people who will use it. If you recruit the wrong people, or don't recruit the right people, then you're getting the wrong data.

What's worse than not seeing how your design works through the eyes of your end users? Seeing it through the eyes of someone who isn't your end user.

A few years ago, I was conducting usability testing on a large content site focused on finding something to do in LA for the weekend. We were looking for participants who were regular users of social network sites and had created some type of user-generated content (e.g., they blogged and wrote reviews for products online).

Most of the participants the recruiting firm sent us fit this profile perfectly. And we learned a great deal from them. One, however, didn't even have an email address. As you might imagine, seeing the site through this person's eyes was essentially useless to us.

The best way to ensure highly qualified participants is to either do your own recruiting with a very detailed screener or hire a professional. Currently, at Messagefirst, we do all of our own recruiting. You can download an example of the screener we use at ✿ rosenfeldmedia.com/downloads/prototyping/Sample_Screener.doc.

Mistake #4: Poorly Formed Research Questions

Formulating research questions correctly is one of the most difficult challenges of usability testing. The key is to get the answer to your question without actually asking the question. Confusing enough?

Let's take the example of the site focused on helping you find something to do in LA for the weekend. The prototype we were testing had content for finding movies, live music, local events, and restaurants.

Now, we could have asked participants to plan dinner and a movie this weekend using the site. That would have been direct and leading. But it wouldn't map to how they plan doing things with friends. It also wouldn't tell us how they used the site, but rather how we wanted them to use the site.

During the initial discussion with participants, we found they *"Looked* for something to do" with friends. That left it open to going to a movie, seeing a live music performance, having drinks, going to dinner, or checking out a music festival.

Instead of asking them "How would you plan dinner and a movie with friends using this site?" we asked "How would you use this site to find something to do with your friends this weekend?"

See the difference? The first is very direct, dinner and a movie, with a fairly predictable outcome. The second is a more open-ended question, allowing them to show us how they would use the site. This is a true test of how the site will perform for them when they are at home, away from us, in the real world, day-to-day.

Mistake #5: Poor Test Moderation

A good usability test moderator is worth his or her weight in ~~gold~~ platinum. Moderating usability tests is a learned skill. In fact, I'd go so far as to call it a craft. Like any craft, it takes a great deal of training, practice, and time. It's not something you pick up overnight. While I believe most people can moderate usability tests, brilliant moderators are rare, and frankly, some people should never be allowed to moderate.

What makes a good moderator? Balance.

A good moderator knows how to balance being a silent fly on the wall with just enough dialogue to keep things moving. They know how to extract the right level of detail without going too deep into the weeds. They know when to let the participant explore and when to pull them back. They know how to get the answer to the question you want without asking the question.

The biggest mistakes made by moderators are talking too much, answering for the participant, and asking direct and leading questions. Sit through a few usability-testing sessions and the skill level of the moderator will become immediately obvious.

The best way to improve your moderating skills is to find a mentor, practice, listen to their critique, and practice some more. You can also try taping yourself and then playing back the audio or videotape to evaluate yourself. You might be surprised what you see and hear.

Mistake #6: Picking the Wrong Method to Communicate Findings and Recommendations

Nobody is going to read that 10–20-page research report you're thinking of writing. Its sole purpose in life is to act as proof that a research study was done. It will remain isolated in the virtual world of bits and bytes. That's it. And yet, you still have to write it.

If they won't read the written report, then how do you communicate the findings? That really depends on the environment and the team you're working with.

Quick review sessions between participants at the end of each day work especially well. These quick review sessions can be used to discuss key takeaways from each participant and to identify patterns as they evolve over the course of the day.

A PowerPoint or Keynote presentation with a summary of the report findings works well. Video clips highlighting key interesting moments during testing are especially effective. It's one thing to hear someone tell you what a participant did during testing. Watching it on video, however, is the next best thing to experiencing it firsthand.

Preparing for a Usability Test

Remember the first guiding principle of prototyping from Chapter 4: "Understand your audience and intent?" That's also the first step in preparing for usability testing. Just like prototyping, this tenet drives every other decision.

Work with your product team to determine the key characteristics and behaviors you're looking for in participants. It's equally important to determine what characteristics and behaviors you *don't* want. Use this information to create a detailed screener.

A sample screener can be found at ⋒ rosenfeldmedia.com/downloads/ prototyping/Sample_Screener.doc, which you can revise for your own needs and use freely.

If you're going to audio or video record the sessions, it's a good idea to provide participants with a waiver and consent form. This gives you the freedom to review the recordings later, while protecting them from their recording ending up on YouTube.

A sample waiver and consent form can be found at ⋔ rosenfeldmedia .com/books.downloads/prototyping/Waiver.doc, which you can revise for your own needs and use freely.

Knowing the intent of your test will inform the scenarios, research questions, and the prototype. These three elements—scenarios, research questions, and prototype—tend to feed off each other.

You might start by designing the scenarios and research questions and using those to drive the prototype. At some point, the prototype will create some additional research questions or possibly even an entirely new scenario you want to test. Just make sure they're in sync with each other in time for testing.

A good rule of thumb is to limit the length of testing sessions to 45–60 minutes. This should be enough time to test five to six key scenarios and not exceed the attention span of your participants. We typically conduct 45-minute sessions with 30-minute breaks in between. Using this format, we're able to conduct six to eight test sessions per day.

Having a 30-minute break between participants provides enough flexibility for participants who show up late (which will happen) or sessions that run longer than 45 minutes (which will also happen).

Additionally, the 30-minute break provides enough time to do a quick debriefing among participants and make any necessary adjustments to the test scenarios or prototype.

Design Test Scenarios

Test scenarios can be either very specific to determine whether or not a participant can access a particular feature on the site, or exploratory in order to gain insight into a participant's overall approach toward solving his or her goal.

In the example Web site used to find something to do in LA for the weekend, the participant's goal wasn't to find a restaurant or even a band. Rather, the participant's goal was to find something entertaining to do with friends. Finding a restaurant and live music was just the process to achieve an enjoyable evening with friends.

Good test scenario design focuses on the goal, while accommodating the activities and the process required to accomplish the goal. A good way to do this is use a combination of an introduction to a scenario with a list of observations or key questions.

If the goal is to find something entertaining to do for the weekend with friends, you might frame the test scenario like this:

"You said earlier that you and your friends were looking for something to do this weekend that might include going out for [dinner, drinks, live music...] and that you wanted to check out that new club [...]. Show me how you might plan that using this Web site."

The [...] are key points where you will insert important contextual information gathered from your opening discussion with the participants.

Next, you could include a few key questions or observations, like the following:

- How do they start (for example, search, browse)?

- Do they look for a place to eat or entertainment first?

- How do they determine which restaurant to go to?

- How do they select what kind of entertainment they want?

- How do they plan (for example, phone calls, SMS, email, twitter)?

- Do they see the map showing locations? Thoughts?

Finally, you'll want to include some type of scoring system for the scenario. We tend to use a sliding scale of 1–5, which is used by both the participant and moderator to rate the scenario.

Test Your Prototype

Soliciting feedback from participants is easier when they're comfortable. One of the tricks I often use is to have the moderator greet the participants, introduce himself (or herself), offer them something to drink, and start a conversation while walking them to the testing room. This gives the moderator a chance to build some rapport with the participants and get them comfortable as quickly as possible.

I've found remote participants are pretty comfortable from the beginning. I imagine it helps being in their own environment instead of coming into a strange place and sitting in a room with a camera pointed at them, while someone watches from another room.

Once they're comfortable, I start with an opening dialogue asking them to describe their experiences related to whatever we're going to test that day. For example, if I wanted to see how they would use a site to find something to do in LA for the weekend, I might ask them to tell me about the last time they planned an evening out with friends.

I might be interested in listening for details like how the planning occurred and if they used email, text messaging, phone calls, or other methods. I might also want to listen for details on what types of activities they considered, such as a movie, dinner, drinks, or going to see a live band.

After you've gathered some information from the opening dialogue, use that information to provide context.

Pretend you have a design challenge to help make their planning easier. Imagine you came up with a concept you want to test called "What's Nearby." The idea is that once someone has found a place of interest, like a restaurant, you show them other places to eat, events, and activities that are nearby. Items nearby would be displayed on a map with star ratings and the number of reviews.

During the opening dialogue, the participant told you he was heading to In and Out Burger and then over to see a local band play. Perfect. You can use that information to frame the scenario and provide real context for him.

I might start off by saying something like, "Remember how you said you had planned to go to In and Out Burger with your friends and then see a live band afterward? Well, I'm going to show you a page and ask you to show me how you might find the In and Out Burger location you want along with anything else close by you might be interested in."

The framing of the scenario includes a couple of key details: real context based on their life and an activity that I can use to test our design concept. Additionally, to keep from being too direct, you'll notice that I asked him to find something "close by" rather than "nearby."

While a subtle nuance, it's a careful balance between having him perform his activity of finding something of interest close to In and Out Burger without giving away the farm.

> **TIP DON'T TOUCH THIS**
>
> If you're testing a prototype that is on a testing or development server, make sure that the development team doesn't touch it the day of testing. I've experienced this once or twice. It's not only frustrating, but also a waste of time for the test participant and the client.

Record Observations and Feedback

Playing the role of moderator and note taker is a daunting task. The best solution is to have one person focus on moderating while another person takes notes remotely. This allows the moderator to focus his or her attention on the participant, while the note taker can focus on taking notes.

When recording notes on your observations, it's best to over-record rather than under-record. If you over-record, you can filter that out during analysis. If you under-record, you may miss a very important piece of information. So, record everything.

As I mentioned earlier, we use a sliding scale of 1–5 to rate each scenario. Both participants and moderators use the same scale. At the end of each scenario, the moderator will ask something like "On a scale of one to five, where one is very difficult and five is very easy, how would you rate finding something to do this weekend in LA?"

The participant's rating is recorded, and the moderator scores the task separately. The moderator's score is not shared with the participant.

The moderator's score should be based on measurable elements like time and effort. An example is something I refer to as pogo-sticking. During pogo-sticking, the participant bounces back and forth, down one path, then back up, then down another, then back up again. Specific metrics like this should be established before testing.

The participant's score is more subjective, qualitative, and a measurement of his or her satisfaction with completing the task. The moderator's score is more objective and quantitative, as it is based on something more measurable, such as time and effort.

Using some type of recording system, like Silverback, Morae, or even a camcorder mounted on a tripod is a great way to ensure that you won't miss anything. If you miss an important detail, you can always go back to the recording and review it. It's also a great way to double-check your notes.

Note-taking methods vary greatly from paper, to Excel spreadsheets, to custom research frameworks.

Morae's has built-in capabilities for note-taking and flagging keyframes during recording. While these features are nice, I've always found the interface and interaction of Morae a bit clunky and awkward. Additionally, Morae doesn't work on a Mac. If you're only concerned about Windows participants, then it's a good solution. Our work often requires testing both Mac and Windows participants. So a non-Mac version of Morae is a deal breaker for us.

Since the quality of our findings is paramount, we try to filter out any variable not directly related to the system we're testing. The experience of Firefox on Windows is not the same as Firefox on the Mac. So we put Mac participants on Macs and Windows participants on Windows.

We use Intel-based iMacs and Silverback to record our audio and video. This solution allows us to run both Mac and Windows on one machine. The screen sharing built into Mac OS X allows us to view the remote machine without the need for additional hardware or software.

When performing remote testing, screen sharing can be done with a number of solutions, including NetMeeting, WebEx, and Adobe Acrobat Connect.

When taking notes, I've found tracking the following three pieces of information make analysis easier:

- **The observation:** Something seen or heard.

- **Time stamp:** At what point in the video did it happen.

- **Tags:** Keywords to describe the observation.

While we've created our own custom framework, which makes capturing and analyzing this information easier, you can record these data points on paper or in a spreadsheet.

Analyze and Determine Next Steps

Most of the time, when I start the analysis process, I have a short list of significant issues that are already at the top of my mind. These are typically things I've seen repeatedly in testing. This short list is just a starting point.

We recently did a number of on-site and remote testing sessions for a client. We knew we had a great deal of information recorded, but weren't really aware of how much until we printed each observation out on a Post-it note and stuck it on our walls. It turns out we had recorded over 1,000 data points.

Seeing 1,000 points of data surrounding us on every wall made it much easier to look at not only the entire set, but also to dig in and identify themes and sub-themes.

It took us several days to work through 1,000 data points, but I don't believe we could have been as effective analyzing both the depth and breadth any other way.

FIGURE 12.1
1,000 points of data.

After you have identified your themes, you can determine the significance of those themes and individual findings within. How do you determine how significant a finding is?

I've seen a number of ways to determine significance. Probably the most common is to base it on frequency (how often it occurred) and severity or learnability (was it a problem every time, or did the severity decrease with continued use?).

I prefer a method I developed a few years ago, which combines the measurement of significance to the customer, value to the business, and technical feasibility of solving the issue (assuming a design solution is available). This method provides a more holistic measurement and a greater ability to prioritize findings.

A Final Word

Several years ago I had a discussion with a usability consultant who referred to summative usability testing—testing that happens at the end. I've never really believed in summative testing, as I don't believe that product development is ever finished. It's an ongoing, living cycle.

Some might find this discouraging—the notion of never being finished. I see it as a great opportunity to continue the learning process, building on past knowledge and experience, iterating and refining my craft by integrating that knowledge and experience.

I hope this book has helped you learn how prototyping is an iterative process. You generate design concepts. You prototype them. You test them. You discover what works, what needs to be refined, and opportunities for new ideas.

I also hope that whether you are just starting out prototyping, or consider yourself a seasoned veteran, you've been able to learn a few tips and tricks to help step up your game, making it easier to sell prototyping to your boss or clients and improve your prototyping skills.

And finally, I'm always interested in learning new methods and techniques myself. If you have a method or technique you'd like to share, I'd love to hear about it. Who knows? Maybe your tip will find its way into a future edition (hint, hint).

Summary

Testing your prototypes is a key step in the prototyping process. Next time you're testing your prototype, keep the following in mind:

- It's a process, not an event.

- Your results are only as good as your participants. Make sure that you're recruiting the right people.

- Good test moderation is a skill that takes years to develop. So practice—a lot.

- Test your prototype before your first day of testing to make sure it works.

- Pick the right method to communicate your findings.

- Video is very powerful.

Index

ACKNOWLEDGMENTS

This book wouldn't have happened without the help and support of a number of people. First, I want to thank Lou Rosenfeld and the advisory board at Rosenfeld Media. I originally went to Lou with three different book topics. It just so happened he picked the one I was probably the least prepared to tackle—poetic how that happens. Thank you Rosenfeld Media for encouraging me to write this book. I really learned a lot in the process.

I hope every author out there is fortunate enough to have an editor who balances tradition with the willingness to try something new. My editor, Marta Justak, did just that. I can't thank Marta enough for working with me on this book and ensuring that it stayed true to my vision.

I spent nine long months doing research for this book. I interviewed vendors and fellow practitioners, asked about their methods and tools, learned new tricks, and even persuaded some of them to contribute an insight or case study.

I'd like to thank the following people for contributing their wisdom to this book: Bill Scott of Netflix, Anders Ramsay an independent UX consultant, David Verba of Adaptive Path, Robert Reimann of frog design, Chris Pallé an independent UX consultant, Victor Hsu of Axure, Scott Mathews of Xplane, Tom Humbarger of iRise, Robert Hoekman, Jr. of Miskeeto, Joe Sokohl of Regular Joe Consulting, Nathan Curtis of EightShapes, Henk Wijnholds and Stefan Wobben of Concept7, Jonathan Baker-Bates of Expedia, and Fred Beecher of Evantage.

I also had a number of brilliant people who reviewed the chapters I wrote on specific methods and tools to make sure they were accurate. I'd like to thank Jeff Patton, an independent UX consultant and Agile coach, for reviewing my paper prototyping chapter, Anders Ramsay for reviewing my chapters on Visio and HTML, Alan Musselman Lead UI Designer and Fireworks Evangelist at Adobe for reviewing my chapter on Fireworks, and Fred Beecher for reviewing my chapter on Axure RP Pro.

And last, but most certainly not least, I'd like to thank my wife, Angela, for gently reminding me that this book wouldn't write itself.

ABOUT THE AUTHOR

Todd Zaki Warfel is the founder and principal designer at Messagefirst, a design consultancy focused on helping companies make products and services that are beautiful, useful, and a pleasure to use. Ask Todd what he does for a living, and he'll tell you he's just a designer. He believes design is a holistic practice, a craft, and like any great artisan, he takes great pride in his craft. He's not one to debate the intricate differences between information architecture, interaction design, persuasion design, or service design—to him, it's all just "Big D" design. Todd sees every problem as a design challenge, and a design challenge is an opportunity to fix something that's broken. He's a fixer. He can't help himself. He's rarely satisfied with the status quo and believes we can always do better, which is one of the reasons he became a designer.

A designer by trade, but not by education, Todd holds degrees in Cognitive Psychology and English Creative Writing. When he graduated college, the Web was still ruled by VAX terminals and books were still printed on paper.

Todd has been designing, building, and breaking things for over 15 years. He has been fortunate enough to design Web sites, Web apps, and other systems for clients such as AT&T Wireless, Bankrate, Citi, Comcast, Cornell, Numara, and New York University. An internally recognized thought leader on research and design, Todd has spoken at conferences and taught workshops around the globe. As a member of the Web Standards Project Education Task Force, Todd leads the effort for their prototyping curriculum.

Todd has a reputation as being a bit of a *foodie* and wine enthusiast. If you ever have the chance to go to dinner with him, chances are it will be a gastronomic adventure you won't soon forget. He also has a professional racing license and hopes to one day get his pilot's license.

Todd currently lives in Philadelphia with his beautiful wife, Angela, their new son, Elijah, and an English bulldog named Duchess. Todd blogs at www.zakiwarfel.com and twitters @zakiwarfel.